俗語・流行語・業界用語…
なにげに使ってるコトバを英語にしてみる

いまどきのニホン語和英辞典

デイヴィッド・P・ダッチャー　編著
研究社辞書編集部　編

研究社

© 2009　KENKYUSHA Co., Ltd.

PRINTED IN JAPAN

まえがき

　この辞典は研究社の『新和英大辞典 第5版』とそのオンライン版 (KOD) の追加語を中心に，現代日本で使われるくだけた表現，俗語，流行語，芸能やスポーツの業界用語を集めたものです．何気なく使っている日本語にも，また英語にも様々な面白い姿があることに興味を持っていただければ幸いです．見出しにはかなり特殊な日本語も多いので，英訳には普通の英語辞書には載っていないような語句も使われていますが，訳の試みの一例とお考えください．

　内容の大半は編集部で構成したものですが，一部の英文は南九州短期大学教授で翻訳家のデイヴィッド・ダッチャー (David Dutcher) 先生にご執筆いただきました．厚く感謝申し上げます．

2009 年 3 月

研究社　辞書編集部

使 い 方

(1) 見出し語は原則として五十音順で,「カー」「ロー」「ビュー」などの伸ばす音は「かあ」「ろお」「びゅう」のように「あ」行に置き換えて順番を決めます.
例:「けいたい」⇨「ケーキ」(「けえき」に置き換える)⇨「ケータイ」(「けえたい」に置き換える)
「メアド」⇨「メイド」⇨「メール」(「めえる」に置き換える)

(2) 丸い括弧 ( ) は省略可能な部分,四角い括弧 [ ] は直前の語句と置き換えが可能な部分を示します.

(3) 英語の訳文・訳語が複数ある場合は「;」で区切ります.語句の前の〔英〕は主に英国で,〔米〕は主に米国で使われることを示します.同様に〔口語〕(くだけた話し言葉),〔俗語〕(やや下品な言葉),〔卑語〕(きわめて下品な言葉) なども表示してあります.

(4) *one's oneself* など斜めの字で書いた部分は,文の主語に対応して my, his, myself, himself のように変わる代名詞です.また ...'s も同様に my, his, Jane's のような所有格を示します.

あ

相方【あいかた】〔一緒に物事をする人〕a [*one's*] partner.
✧漫才で**相方**をつとめる　partner ... [act as ...'s partner] in a *manzai* (comic duo). ★最初の partner ... は「…とパートナーを組む」を意味する動詞．

アイコラ〔アイドル・コラージュの略．女性アイドルや女優の顔だけをヌード写真などと合成した画像〕a composite photograph of a film or TV idol's head attached to another woman's body; a faked [doctored] photograph (of a young female celebrity).

愛妻弁当【あいさいべんとう】a packed lunch (lovingly) prepared by *one's* wife; a packed lunch made by *one's* beloved wife's fair hands.

あいた(た)ー，あちゃー ouch; ow; oops; uh-oh; Oh, no!

◇「金が無いから彼女の誕生日に自作の歌プレゼントしたらふられた」「**あいたー！** やっちまったなあ」"I was out of money so I wrote a song as a birthday present for my girlfriend, but it pissed her off and she dumped me." "Ouch! You sure blew it."

◇友達の悪口を間違って本人にメールしちまった．**あいたたた〜！** Uh-oh! Big trouble! By mistake, I sent that text message to the very acquaintance I bad-mouthed in it.

◇**あちゃー**，また寝坊だ！ Darn it!〔Oh Christ〕I've overslept again! Now I'm in for it.

アイテム 〔必要とされる小道具・必携品〕a requisite (item).

◇大学に合格して春から一人暮らしを始める君，こんな**アイテム**を揃えよう．So you have graduated from university and will begin living on your own this spring. Here are the items you will need to assemble.

◇必須**アイテム** an indispensable item.

◇レア・**アイテム** a rare [an unusual] item. ★⇨レア

アイドリング・ストップ 〔停車中のアイドリングをしないこと〕stopping [switching off] the engine when a vehicle is not moving; "idling stop."

◇**アイドリング・ストップ**宣言車 a vehicle that is taking part in an "idling stop" campaign;〔車体の掲示〕This Vehicle Shuts Off Its Engine When Stopped.

アイドル 〔人気のある若手芸能人〕a teenage star; a popular teenage entertainer; a teen pop star; a teenage entertainer idolized by the young; a (teen) heartthrob.

◇若者の**アイドル** a teenage entertainer [singer, comedian] idol-

ized by the young; an idol of young people [the young].
  ◇あの歌手はむかし若者の**アイドル**だった．That singer used to be idolized by the young.
  ◇お茶の間の**アイドル** a teenage star widely known through television; a household darling.
  ◇**アイドル**から大人の俳優へ脱皮する develop from a teenage star into a full-fledged [mature] actor [actress].
  ◇**アイドル**歌手 a (teenage) pop star; a singing idol; an idolized singer.
  ◇**アイドル**・ファンド〔新人アイドルに投資する金融商品〕the (Pinup) Idol Fund; a fund investing in the career of selected aspiring media stars. ★⇨アイコラ

愛の鞭【あいのむち】 a whip tempered with love
  ◇彼女のために**愛の鞭**を振るう be strict with her out of love for her.
  ◇子供を思う気持ちからあえて**愛の鞭**を振るった．Out of our love for them we were strict with our children.
  ◇鬼コーチがしごくのも**愛の鞭**だ．Our hard-driving coach wields a whip tempered with love.

アウェー〔相手チームのホームグラウンドで対戦すること〕
  ◇いくら人気のあるチームでも**アウェー**の試合では集客力が落ちる．No matter how popular it is, a team's drawing power diminishes in away games.
  ◇**アウェー**で勝つのは難しい．It's hard to win away from your home ground [field, court].

赤い糸【あかいいと】
◇運命の赤い糸 the romantic [instinctive] thread of fate (linking a man and woman)
◇彼と私は運命の赤い糸で結ばれているの. He and I are bound, each to the other, by a red thread of destiny.

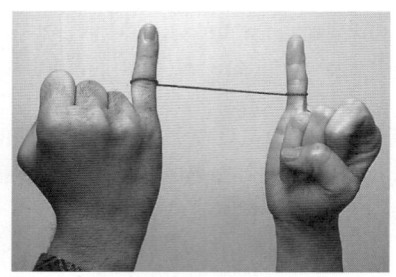

赤信号【あかしんごう】a red light
◇赤信号, みんなで渡れば怖くない. Red light! If we all cross together what can they do.;〔多数なら安全〕There's safety in numbers.

開かずの【あかずの】never opened; unopened; forbidden.
◇開かずの間 an unopened room; a room that is never [that has never been] opened; a room that is kept (permanently) closed
◇事件以来そこは開かずの間になっている. The room has been kept closed [Nobody has been allowed into the room] since the crime was committed there.
◇開かずの門[扉] an unopened gate [door]; a gate [door] that is never [that has never been] opened; a door [gate] that is kept (permanently) closed
◇開かずの踏切 a〔米〕grade [〔英〕level] crossing that always seems to be closed.

垢擦り【あかすり】
〔垢をこすり落とすこと〕scrubbing [rubbing] grime off the skin;〔あかすりの道具〕(布) a rough-textured cloth to remove grime from the skin; (軽石) a pumice stone; (へちま) a loofa(h).
◇韓国式**垢擦り** Korean-style *akasuri*.

赤ちゃん【あかちゃん】a baby.
◇**赤ちゃん**言葉(を使う) (use) baby language; the (sort of) words [language] a baby uses.
◇**赤ちゃん**ポスト〔さまざまな事情で子育てができない親が新生児を匿名で託す設備〕a baby post (box); a baby hatch [drop-off]; a foundling wheel.

赤髭先生【あかひげせんせい】
〔山本周五郎原作、黒澤明監督の映画に登場する患者中心の自己犠牲的な医師〕Doctor Red Beard; the altruistic Edo-period doctor, featured in the novel by Yamamoto Shugoro and the film by Kurosawa Akira, who devotes his life to treating the poor.

赤丸急上昇【あかまるきゅうじょうしょう】
◇この商品[タレント]は今**赤丸急上昇**中だ．This「product's [TV personality's] popularity is growing by leaps and bounds.

赤目【あかめ】
〔ストロボ撮影で目が赤く写ること〕red eye; the red-eye effect.
◇**赤目**防止機能 red-eye reduction.

あ(っ)かんべえ，アカンベー
◇…に**あかんべえ**をする make a face at ... by pulling down the lower lid of one eye, as a gesture of derision or rejection.
◇**アカンベー**だ．Nuts to you!（★ nuts は「バカ，うるせえ，

チェッ！」の意); Buzz off! (★「うせろ，あっち行け」の意)

秋色【あきいろ】
〔秋らしい色〕an autumn(al) color;〔米〕a fall color.
◇すっかり**秋色**に染まった山〔紅葉しているさま〕mountains dyed [ablaze, decked out] in autumnal [fall] colors.
◇**秋色**メーク cosmetics in autumn [fall] color.

アキバ系，秋葉系【あきばけい】
〔東京の秋葉原に集まるアニメ・ゲーム・パソコンなどのオタク〕(anime) geeks frequenting Akihabara in Tokyo; "Akihabara geeks."

空き家【あきや】
〔付き合う異性がいない状態〕singleness; celibacy.
◇私ここ３年**空き家**なの．I've been unattached for the past three years.; I haven't had a boyfriend [gone with anyone] for three years.

諦めムード【あきらめムード】
a mood of resignation.
◇彼がすべての女性に同様の仕打ちを加えているのを知って彼女の怒りは**あきらめムード**に変わった．Her mood changed from one of anger to one of resignation as she realized that he treated all women in the same way.
◇チームには半ば**あきらめムード**がただよっていた．A mood approaching resignation hung over the team.

握手会【あくしゅかい】
〔アイドルなどとファンの〕a handshake session.

悪玉コレステロール【あくだまコレステロール】
the "bad cholesterol." ★正式名は「低密度リポ蛋白(質)」(low-density

lipoprotein, 略称 LDL).

あけおめ 〔あけましておめでとうの略〕HNY (Happy New Year)
★メールなどで使う略語.

顎足付き【あごあしつき】〔食事代・交通費付き〕
◇あご足付きの招待旅行 a complimentary trip [tour] with all expenses paid; an all-expenses-paid [all-in] (complimentary) trip; a (complimentary) trip for which everything is [travel and all meals are] paid (by the company).
◇今度のアルバイトはあご足付きだ. The new part-time job covers food and travel expenses.;〔口語〕This part-time job has meals and transport thrown in.

朝立ち【あさだち(する)】〔朝の勃起〕(have [get]) a morning erection [〔俗語〕morning wood].

朝一【あさいち】 ⇨ごごいち

脚[足]タレ【あしタレ】〔広告などで足だけ写るタレント〕a leg [foot] model.

足壺【あしつぼ】, 足裏【あしうら】
◇足壺マッサージする, 足裏の壺を押す press the points on the sole [bottom] of /one's/ foot.
◇足裏健康法 sole therapy; reflexology (on the soles of the feet).
◇足裏マッサージ (a) sole massage.

あそこがかゆい
◇先生, あそこがかゆいんです.〔女性が〕Doctor, I've got an itch in a sensitive place.;〔男性が〕Doctor, my crotch is itchy.;

Doctor, I've got an itch in my crotch. ★⇨デリケートゾーン

アダルト 〔成人向けの・ポルノの〕 pornographic; erotic; dirty; sex;〔口語〕porn; blue; adult;〔大人の・成熟した〕adult; grown-up; mature.

◇アダルトな感じの服装をしている be dressed in a grown-up-looking way; have adult-looking clothes on.

◇アダルトなムードのバー a bar with a settled [calm, quiet] atmosphere.

◇アダルト・ショップ a sex [porn, skin] shop.

◇アダルト・チルドレン 〔精神的に大人になりきれていない人〕 adults who are morally immature.

◇アダルト・ビデオ (an) adult video; (a) pornographic [〔口語〕porn] video; a sex [dirty] video.

◇アダルト・ファッション fashion(s) [design(s)] for adults; adult fashion(s).

◇アダルト・ゲーム an adult game.

◇アダルト・コンテンツ 〔ウェブサイトなどの〕 adult [pink] content.

◇アダルト・サイト an adult (Web) site.

◇アダルト番組 〔ネットや電話での〕 adult entertainment service [(テレビの) program].

◇(ネット上などでの)有料アダルト番組 paid adult entertainment content.

あちゃー ⇨あいたた

熱い【あつい】

◇あの二人は熱い仲だ. They are sweet on [deeply in love with] each other.

◇お熱いところをたっぷり見せつけられた. They were rather

too demonstrative in their expression of love.
★感嘆詞の「あつっ！」「あちち！」「アッチッチ！」は英語では「痛い！」と同じ ouch! でよい．

アッカンベー　⇨あかんべえ

厚底靴［ブーツ，サンダル］【あつぞこぐつ［ブーツ，サンダル］】 platform shoes [boots, sandals].

あっちむいてほい　*atchi muite hoi*; a "look that way" game; a game in which two people play a round of rock-paper-scissors [*janken*], the winner points at the loser's face and moves his or her finger quickly up, down, left or right while saying "atchi muite hoi," and the loser simultaneously moves his or her face in one of those four directions, losing again if the winner's finger and the loser's face move in the same direction.

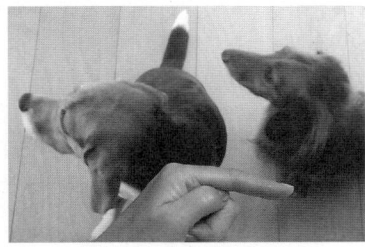

あっぷあっぷ〔精一杯〕
◇わが社は不景気で金が回らず**あっぷあっぷ**している．As a result of the recession our firm has a cash-flow problem, and is struggling to survive.
◇あの会社の経営は**あっぷあっぷ**の状態だ．That firm is drowning in red ink [on the verge of going under, in real difficulties, in big trouble]. ★⇨いっぱいいっぱい

アップする
〔ウォーミングアップする〕warm up; limber up;〔アップロードする〕upload. ★⇨とうこう

後追い【あとおい】〔模倣〕imitating; an imitation.
◇(…の)**後追い**自殺[心中] suicide committed to join ... [*one's beloved*] in death.
◇これは1年前に大当たりしたテレビゲームの**後追い**だ．This is an imitation of the TV game that was a big hit the year before.
◇**後追い**商品 an imitation [a copycat] product. ★⇨あやかりしょうひん

アニメ(ーション)
〔アニメの技法〕animation;〔アニメ作品〕an animated cartoon.
◇クレイ・アニメ(ーション)〔粘土の人形などをコマ撮りしたアニメ〕clay animation; claymation.
◇**アニメ・キャラ** an animated cartoon character.
◇**アニメ映画** an animated cartoon; an animation.
◇少女向け小説の**アニメ化** animation of a story for young girls.
◇**アニメ作家** an animator; an animated cartoon producer. ★⇨オタク

COLUMN

anime, manga はもはや英語？

「アニメ」に相当する最も普通の英語は animation や (car)toon, 他に animated film（アニメ映画）など．ただ現在は海外に日本のアニメファンが増えた結果，anime（発音は「**ア**ニメイ」に近い）という表記も特にインターネット上ではかなり使われるようになっている．「漫画」もひとコマ漫画は (car)toon, 続き漫画は comics, comic strip [book] などが普通の言い方だが，日本のアニメや漫画は japanimation, また日本語からそのまま manga と呼ばれることも多い．
ちなみに世界最大の英語辞典であるオックスフォード英語辞典（OED）のオンライン版にも anime, manga が収録されており，manga の説明では「丁寧に細部まで描き込まれた絵柄をもち，たいていは星のようにキラキラした大きな瞳の人物が登場し，SFやファンタジーものが多く，時に暴力的あるいはエロチックな描写も見られる．」などと解説している．ウェブ上の百科辞典として有名なウィキペディア（Wikipedia）はもともと英語版から始まったものだが，数多くの日本アニメ，漫画の記事があり，日本語版より詳しい情報が載っていることさえある．動画投稿サイトとして有名な YouTube 他の動画サイトでも英語やスペイン語で解説や字幕や吹き替えの付いた日本アニメ画像が無数に見られる．⇨コスプレ

脂取り紙【あぶらとりがみ】〔顔の〕facial oil-blotting paper; face paper.

アポなし訪問[取材]【アポなしほうもん[しゅざい]】an unscheduled visit [interview]; a visit [an interview] without an appointment.

甘噛み【あまがみ】〔ペットがじゃれついて軽く噛むこと〕a love nip

◇ペットの子犬が彼女の人さし指を**甘噛み**した Her puppy gave her a love nip on her forefiger.

あやかり商品【あやかりしょうひん】goods (sold by being) linked to something famous or popular.
◇町はオリンピックの**あやかり商品**であふれていた．The town was flooded with Olympic-related goods. ★⇨あとおい

荒らし【あらし】〔ネット上の掲示板などで悪質ないたずら・妨害行為をする人〕a troll;〔その行為〕trolling. ◇**荒らし**をする troll. ◇掲示板**荒らし**〔人〕a bulletin board troll;〔行為〕bulletin board trolling.

アラサー〔around 30（アラウンド-サーティー）の略．2006年ごろに30歳前後となった女性世代〕a cohort of women who turned thirty in or around 2006 and who share a range of demographic fashion information, such as baggy white socks and hair dyed brown, that were the vogue among high-school students in the mid-1990s.

アラフォー〔around 40（アラウンド-フォーティー）の略．2008年ごろに40歳前後となった女性世代〕a cohort of women who turned forty in or around 2008 and who were the first to benefit from the Equal-Opportunity Employment Law for Men and Women, which came into force in 1986. The term occurs in dis-

cussions of fashion, generational shift, and purchasing power.

ありえない，ありえねー 〔信じられないほどひどい〕 That's not possible.; I don't believe it.
◇あいつ幹事のくせに合コンの最中にずっとメールしてやがんの．マジ**ありえねー**よ．The guy organizes a party for singles but the whole time all he does is text-message other people. I don't believe it. I mean, is he for real?!
◇うちの学校は今時ケータイ所有禁止という**ありえない**校則がある．It's hard to believe, in this day and age, that my school still has a rule prohibiting cell phones.
◇顔は可愛いのにファッションが**ありえない**女だ．She's pretty but her taste in clothes is totally off the wall.

あるあるネタ 〔よくある体験で笑いを取るネタ〕 a type of story that strikes a common chord of humor with the experiences of many other people; a conversation topic that evokes a sympathetic chuckle from everyone.

安近短【あんきんたん】 〔安い費用で近場の観光地に短い日程で旅行すること〕 taking a short, inexpensive trip to a nearby location.

安全牌【あんぜんぱい】 〔麻雀で〕 a safe play; a (mah-jongg [mahjong]) tile that can safely be thrown away without any benefit to *one's* opponents; 〔危険がないこと〕 a safe bet [choice].
◇彼なら**安全牌**だ．He is a safe choice.

アンチエイジング 〔抗老化・抗加齢〕 antiaging.
◇**アンチエイジング**医療 (an) antiaging therapy [treatment].
◇**アンチエイジング**・ケア antiaging care.

い

いいとこ取り【いいとこどり】
◇彼は都会生活と田舎暮らしのいいとこ取りをねらったのだがうまく行かなかった. He tried to get the best of both city life and country life, but he couldn't manage to do so.
◇これはスキーと温泉と新酒と旬の魚を日帰りで楽しむいいとこ取りの計画だ. Skiing, hot springs, newly brewed sake and fish at their best: with this plan you get [can pick, can take your pick of] the best of everything and enjoy it all on a one-day visit.

イエ(ー)イ 〔"やったぞ"という意の発声〕Yeah!; Done it!; Olé!

言え(て)る【いえ(て)る】
◇「いくらあせっても結果は同じだよ」「それは言えてるな」"No matter how much you rush things, the result will be the same." "That's probably true."
◇「あの男, 刑事みたいな目つきで僕らを見たぞ」「言えてる!」"That guy looked at us like a detective." "You can say that again!"

家電【いえでん】〔携帯電話に対して, 各家庭の固定電話〕a fixed-line [traditional, conventional] phone [telephone]; a wired telephone[phone].

行く 【いく，イク】〔セックスで絶頂に達する〕come；〔現実から遊離している〕be somewhere else.
　◇女[男]を行かせる make a woman [man] come.
　◇行く！ I'm coming!
　◇完全に行っちゃってる小説 a novel that is completely beyond the pale.
　◇奴に今話しかけても無駄だよ．ありゃあどっか行っちゃってる目だ． There's no point in talking to him now. You can see in his eyes that he's somewhere else.
　◇次もこの手で行くとしよう． I think we should go with this (move) the next time, too.
　◇今日は久しぶりに一杯行こうじゃないか． It's been quite a while since we've been for a drink together, so let's go out tonight.
　◇〔撮影で〕さあ，本番行ってみよう． Right, this time it's a take.

イケイケ 〔慎重さを欠いた積極性・抑制のきかない奔放性〕
　◇イケイケムード a go-go mood
　◇イケイケギャル a go-go girl
　◇イケイケドンドンの拡大路線 go-go expansionism.

イケてる 〔いかしている，かっこいい〕good-looking; nice; cute; cool.

イケメン
a handsome [good-looking] man [〔口語〕guy]; 〔口語〕a hunk.

いじられキャラ
✧あいつは職場[クラス]の**いじられキャラ**で，しょっちゅうドジを踏んでは笑いを取っている．He's the office jokester [class clown]—always ready to do a pratfall to draw a laugh. ★⇨きゃく

痛い【イタい】
✧電車の中で大声で演説してるかなり**イタい**奴がいた．There was some prissy, hypocritical, loudmouthed, do-gooder spreading his message on the train.
✧イケメン気取りの**イタい**連中だ．They're just prissy guys trying to look sharp.
✧女の子がサッカーやるのは無作法だって？ 今時何**痛い**こと言ってんの？ It's bad manners for girls to play football, you say? Where are you coming from, the Dark Ages?
✧ただの雑種犬の名前が「エカテリーナ2世」ってちょっと**イタく**ないか？ Isn't it a bit pretentious [highfalutin] to name a common mongrel Ekaterina the Second?

痛車【いたしゃ】
〔アニメやゲームのキャラクターのシールやイラストを貼り付け，あるいは塗装した自動車〕a car decorated with [covered in] (illustrations of) anime characters.

一芸入試【いちげいにゅうし】
an entrance exam for a university giving preference to those with nonacademic talents or abilities.

イチゴ大福 【イチゴだいふく】 a strawberry *daifuku*; a *daifuku* containing strawberry.

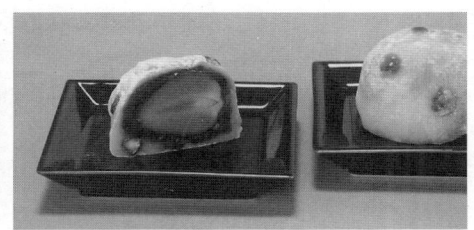

一卵性親子 【いちらんせいおやこ】〔非常に仲のよい親子, 特に母と娘〕a parent [mother] and child who have a very close relationship.
❖彼女と母親は**一卵性親子**みたいだ. She and her mother are (as) thick as thieves. ★ thick as thieves は「泥棒仲間のように結束が固い」の意. thick と thieves (thief の複数形) はどちらも語の最初の発音が同じで, 日本語の「結構毛だらけ猫灰だらけ」のように調子のよい語感を生み出す一種のしゃれにもなっている.

一話完結 【いちわかんけつ】 ⇨かんけつ

一気(飲み) 【いっき(のみ)】 drinking down [downing] a jug of beer in one go; drinking a large glass (of beer) without pausing for breath;〔口語〕chugalugging.
❖**一気飲み**する (drink) down a large glass of beer in one go; drink a large glass (of beer) without pausing for breath;〔口語〕chugalug. ★ chugalug(ging) は, 液体を飲むときの「グビグビ, ゴックンゴックン」という擬音語を動詞化したもの.
❖彼は大ジョッキのビールを**一気**に飲み干した. He drained the tankard of beer in one.

◇さあ，**一気**に飲もう．Right! Bottoms up!; Let's drain our glasses.
◇**一気**コール a call to drink up; "Bottoms up!" ★ bottoms up は「杯の底 (bottom) を上にして (逆さまにして) 飲み干せ」の意味．

イッシッシ，いひひ，うひひ 〔ずるそうな笑い声〕the sound of gleeful chuckles; tee-hee; hee-hee(-hee).
◇彼は気味悪く**イヒヒ**と笑った．He snickered [sniggered] unpleasantly.
◇宝くじの2等に当選して「**うひひひ**！ やったね！」と歓声を上げた．When he won second prize in a lottery, he shouted for joy: "Whee! I won!"

いっ(ちゃっ)てる ⇨いく

一通【いっつう】〔一方通行〕one-way traffic; 〔標識〕One Way. ★ "DO NOT ENTER" や "WRONG WAY" も同じ意味の標識．
◇**一通**の標識 a one-way sign; 〔標識自体をさして〕a "ONE WAY" sign.
◇このあたりは道が狭くて，**一通**のところが多い．In this area roads are narrow and in many places traffic is only one way.
◇彼は**一通**の道をバックで逆走した．He drove in reverse up a one-way street.
◇〔車に乗っていて〕あそこは**一通**だから入れないよ．That's a one-way street so you can't go in there.

一杯一杯【いっぱいいっぱい】
◇これだけの月給では**いっぱいいっぱい**です．I can just barely get by on this meager salary.
◇もうこのお値段で**一杯一杯**です．This is absolutely the lowest price I can offer.

◇この幅だったら，あそこに**一杯一杯**で入るんじゃないかな．A piece of this width might just barely fit into that space.
◇**いっぱいいっぱい**の生活が長く続いて，彼女は疲れ切っている．She is completely exhausted [burnt out] from working flat out [on overdrive] for so long.

一発芸【いっぱつげい】 a quick trick.

一発屋【いっぱつや】 〔堅実さに欠けるがたまに大きなことをやってのける人〕a one-shot speculator;〔俗語〕a one-time johnny;〔野球の〕a batter who always swings for the seats (and occasionally succeeds); a home-run hitter;〔一回だけ活躍して姿を消す芸能人など〕a flash in the pan.
◇最近は1曲だけヒットして消え去る**一発屋**の歌手が多い．Recently there have been a lot of flash-in-the-pan singers who disappear from the public eye after just one hit song.

一般ピープル【いっぱんピープル】 ⇨パンピー

いひひ ⇨イッシッシ

今カノ【いまカノ】, 今カレ【いまカレ】 *one's* (current) girl [boy] friend. ★⇨もとカノ，もとカレ，かのじょ，かれし

いまさら感【いまさらかん】
◇**いまさら感**が漂う[ぬぐえない]話題だ．Who cares about that subject [issue, problem] anymore?; That's all yesterday's news.; That subject [issue] is pretty dated

イメチェン, イメージチェンジ a change in *one's* image; a change of image; an image-change.

イモ

❖**イメチェンする** change [alter] *one's* (public) image; change the image.
❖ **イメチェンを図る** try [aim] to change *one's* (public) image; try [aim] to acquire a new (public) image.
❖彼女は髪を短く切ってすっかり**イメージチェンジ**した．Cutting her hair short has completely changed her image.; You'd think she was a different person since she had her hair cut short.

芋【イモ】〔やぼったい人〕an unrefined person; a person with no refinement [sophistication];〔男〕a clod; a bumpkin.
❖あいつは**イモ**だからこういう服は似合わないだろう．He's got no style, so these clothes wouldn't suit him.
❖そんな帽子のかぶり方をすると**イモ**にいちゃん[ねえちゃん]みたいだぞ．If you wear your hat like that, people will think you're fresh [you've just come] up from the country.

芋い【イモい】⇨ださい

癒し系【いやしけい】something to do with healing; a therapy.
❖癒し系の音楽 healing music.

色ち【いろち】, 色違い【いろちがい】variation in color.
❖彼と彼女は**色違い**のポロシャツを着ている．He and she are wearing matching polo shirts of different colors.
❖私はこれの**色違い**を持っているわ．I have the same thing in a different color.
❖これはそれの**色違い**だね．同じ柄だもの．The design is the same, see? This is just a variation of that in a different color.
❖この小皿は**色違い**で5枚組になっています．These small plates come in color-varied sets of five.

イントロクイズ

イントロクイズ〔前奏だけで曲名を当てるクイズ〕a game in which players must name a tune after listening only to the openingbars; a game of guessing the name of a musical piece after hearing the opening bars.
◇ラジオの**イントロクイズ** a radio intro quiz

う

上から目線【うえからめせん】
◇「まあ悪くない出来なんじゃないの,君にしては」「うわ,何その**上から目線**?」 "It's not bad at all, considering you wrote it yourself." "Don't condescend to me [patronize me]."

受ける【ウケる】
〔…に人気を得る〕appeal to . . . ; be popular [a big hit] among [with] . . . ; win [enjoy] popularity; go down well with . . . ; be well received; 〔口語〕catch on with . . . ; succeed; 〔口語〕go over well.

◇それ超**ウケる**〜!〔面白い話を聞いた時の誉め言葉〕Wow, far-out!; Out-a-sight!; Right on!; Groovy!; Hey, I can really groove on that. ★far-out, out-a-sight (out-of-sight の崩れた形) は「(目に見えないほど)遠く離れた,現実離れした,ありえないほど面白い」の意. right on は「(笑いのツボに)どんぴしゃ」, groovy, groove は「溝 (groove) にはまる,ツボに入る」が原義.

◇そのギャグは全然**受け**なかった. The gag didn't go over well at all.

◇このジョークは学生たちに大いに**受けた**. This joke made a big hit with students.

◇この舞台はあらゆる世代の人に**受ける**と思います. I think this stage presentation will appeal to people of all generations.

◇全米で大ヒットしたこの映画は日本でも**受ける**だろう. This movie [film] was a big hit in the US, and I think it'll be well received in Japan, too.

◇この小説はきっと多くの人に**受ける**に相違ない. This novel is sure to appeal to a lot of people.

◇この漫画は小学生の間ですごく**受けて**いる. This cartoon is

extremely popular among primary school children.

ウザい，ウザったい be a (big) nuisance;〔口語〕be a (big) pain in the neck; be irritating [bothersome]; be in the way.

うだうだ，ウダウダ
◇(…のことを)うだうだ言う go on and on about . . . ; drivel on and on
◇うだうだする，うだうだと過ごす idle away the time; loaf; dawdle
◇何もしないでうだうだしてるなら手伝え．If you're not doing anything and just idling away the time, give me a hand.
◇つまらないことをいつまでもうだうだ言うな．Stop going [driveling] on and on and on about inconsequential things [trivia].

打たれ弱い【うたれよわい】be a defeatist; (have) a defeatist attitude; give up [collapse at] the first sign of opposition

宇宙人【うちゅうじん】〔奇人・理解不能の人〕a person from another planet.
◇あいつは何を考えているのかさっぱりわからない，私にとってはまるで宇宙人だ．I've no idea what he's thinking; as far as I'm concerned he might as well be from another planet.

ウヒヒ ⇨イッシッシ

馬なり【うまなり】〔競馬で手綱を締めず自由に走らせること〕giving a horse free rein.
◇その馬は調教では馬なりでいいタイムを出す．In training, that horse makes good time when given a free rein.

うら…

◇馬なりに走らせる give a horse free rein; let a horse have its head.

裏… 【うら…】〔陰の〕behind-the-scenes;〔非正規の〕unofficial; informal; unauthorized.

◇裏サイト〔インターネット上の〕(非公式の) an unofficial (Web) site;（あやしげな）a dubious (Web) site;〔口語〕a dodgy [fishy] (Web) site;（違法な）an illegal (Web) site.

◇学校裏サイト a dubious (Web) site used by the students at a school.

◇裏献金 an undeclared [a concealed, an illicit] donation [contribution].

◇裏合意 (a) secret [behind-the-scenes] agreement.

◇裏収入 (a) secret income;〔申告しない〕(an) undeclared income;〔違法の〕(an) illegal income.

◇裏情報 underground information.

◇裏番長 a hidden [secret] boss [leader]. ★⇨うらピース，うらメニュー，うらビデオ，うらわざ

浦島太郎 【うらしまたろう】(a) Rip van Winkle. ★アメリカの作家ワシントン・アーヴィングの物語に登場する人物で，山の中で20年間眠り続けた後で目覚めた．

◇20年ぶりに帰国したら，東京はすっかり変わっていて，**浦島太郎**になった気分だった． When I came back to Japan after twenty years away, Tokyo was so completely changed I felt like Rip van Winkle [a stranger].

裏ピース 【うらピース】〔相手に手の甲を向けたピースサイン〕a backhanded V-sign; any of various V-sign poses assumed, largely by young women, for group pictures taken in *Purikura* photo booths or by cell-phone.

裏ビデオ【うらビデオ】a black-market [uncensored] pornographic video.

恨めしい【うらめしい】
✧うらめしや〔幽霊などが〕Wooooo . . . I'm gonna get you-u-u.
★I'm going to get you.((呪い)殺してやるぞ)を恨めしげに言ったもの.

裏メニュー【うらメニュー】〔メニューには載っていないが常連客などにだけ出す特別料理〕an off-the-menu dish offered only to the regular clientele of a restaurant.

裏技, ウラ技【うらわざ】〔TV ゲームなどの秘密文字列〕a cheat (code);〔秘技〕a trick of the trade;〔公には認められていない方法〕sharp practice; an unscrupulous maneuver;〔家事や日常生活上のちょっとした工夫・知恵〕household hints; ideas for the home; household tips and tricks.
✧この攻略本にはこのゲームの**裏技**がたくさん載っている．This "how-to-win" manual has a lot of tricks of the trade of [for] this computer game.
✧格安チケットを**裏技**で手に入れる gain access to [〔口語〕get hold of] bargain-price tickets by a secret ploy.

◇この2つのボタンを同時に押すと**裏技**を使うことができる．If you press these two buttons at the same time, you can use a trick of the trade.

◇こうなったらとっておきの**裏技**を出すしかないな．In this situation all you can do is come up with your super-special trick of the trade.

ウリセン，売り専 〔男性同性愛者相手の売春宿〕a gay whorehouse; a gay brothel; 〔男娼〕a male prostitute; a (male) hustler; a rentboy.

うるうる

◇**うるうる**する be teary-eyed; have tears in *one's* eyes.

◇彼の演説は感動的なもので，彼女も目を**うるうる**させながらそれを聞いていた．His speech was moving, and she listened to it teary-eyed.

◇あこがれの映画スターのサインをもらった彼女は感極まって**うるうる**状態だった．Overcome with emotion after getting the autograph of the movie star of her dreams, she was teary-eyed.

浮気【うわき】〔不貞〕extramarital sex; unfaithfulness; inconstancy; fickleness; wantonness; infidelity; 〔移り気〕capriciousness; caprice.

◇**浮気**な〔移り気な〕capricious; fickle; whimsical; flighty; skittish; 〔淫奔な〕flirtatious; wanton; 〔不貞な〕unchaste; unfaithful; inconstant.

◇彼は**浮気**な男ではない．He is not the type to be untrue.

◇**浮気**する〔既婚者が〕be unfaithful to *one's* wife [husband]; have an affair [extramarital sex] with . . . ; betray [deceive] *one's* wife [husband]; 〔一般的に〕see another woman [man]; see somebody else; 〔口語〕cheat on *one's* spouse [girlfriend, boy-

friend]; run [play] around with …;〔ふたまたかける〕two-time.
◇あの男は**浮気**するタイプじゃない．He's not the type who runs around [to play around] (with other women).
◇今年は**浮気**して，別のチームを応援するつもりです．This year I plan to transfer my affections to another team.
◇彼の**浮気**がばれた．His infidelity was found out (by his wife).
◇彼女は夫の度重なる**浮気**に困っている．She doesn't know what to do about her husband's (constant) running around [philandering].
◇持ち前の**浮気**の虫は封じようもない．There's no cure for a born playboy [philanderer] like him.
◇**浮気**は男の甲斐性(かいしょう)なんて，時代錯誤も甚だしい．For him to say that having an affair shows a man's true worth is way out of step with the times.
◇**浮気**癖 a habit of being unfaithful [philandering,〔口語〕cheating on one's spouse, running around].
◇**浮気者**〔男〕a playboy; a woman [〔口語〕skirt] chaser; a womanizer; a Don Juan; a philanderer;〔女〕a flirt; a fickle woman; a loose [〔口語〕an easy] woman;〔口語〕a vamp;〔ふたまたかける人〕two-timer.
◇**浮気**相手 an illicit lover; a partner in an adulterous love affair.
◇**浮気**調査 an infidelity investigation.
◇**浮気**現場を押さえる catch an adulterer in the act.

ウンコ座り ⇨ヤンキーずわり

うんたらかんたら ⇨なんだかんだ

え

エア… 〔身振りだけでやること〕
◇エアギターをやる play (the) air guitar; put on an air-guitar performance
◇エアテニスをやる play a set of air-ball tennis

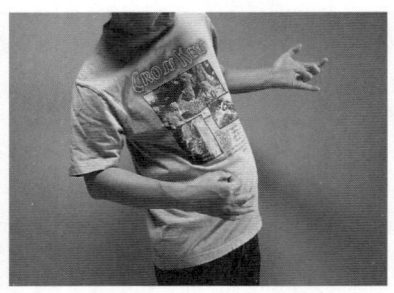

AV 【えーぶい】〔視聴覚〕audiovisual;〔アダルトビデオ〕(a) porno(graphic) [(an) adult] video.
◇AV 教材 audovisual (teaching) materials.
◇AV 女優 a female video porn star; a porno actress; an actress in X-rated videos.
◇AV ギャル a pornstar
◇AV 男優 a male video porn star; a porno actor; an actor in X-rated videos.

駅ナカ 【えきナカ】〔駅構内の小売り店〕a retail shop inside a station; an in-station store [shop].
◇駅ナカビジネス (an) in-station business.

エグい 〔思いやりがなく冷酷な〕sharp; biting.

✧彼女はやさしそうな顔をしているが言うことはかなりえぐい．She looks kind but her words are biting.

✧記者たちのえぐい質問に彼女はとうとう泣きだした．She finally burst into tears at the reporters' sharp questions.

エコノミークラス症候群【エコノミークラスしょうこうぐん】economy class syndrome;〔医学用語〕deep vein thrombosis (略 DVT).

S【エス】, M【エム】〔サドとマゾ〕sadist and masochist;〔SM 嗜好〕sadomasochism. ★⇨じょおうさま

✧彼女が彼氏を顎でこき使うから最初はびっくりしたけど，「どS」と「どM」のカップルだからあれでうまくいってるんだ．It had startled me to see her ordering her man about with a wave of her chin, but it turns out their opposed hardcore S&M tendencies make it a perfect match.

エチケット袋【エチケットぶくろ】〔飛行機酔いなどのための〕an air sickness bag; a sick bag;〔口語〕a puke [barf] bag.

エッチ

✧エッチな dirty; dirty-minded; obscene; indecent; lewd; obsessed with sex.

✧エッチな話はやめて．〔口語〕Watch your mouth.; None of your smuttiness [dirty talk].

✧あの人エッチね．He is a (terrible) lecher, isn't he!; He's got a dirty mind, hasn't he?; He's filthy-minded.

✧きゃー，エッチ！ のぞかないでよ．Don't look, you horrible lecher [filthy creep, dirty old man]!

✧…とエッチする have sex with ....

絵手紙【えてがみ】a plain postcard illustrated with a drawing by the sender to which are added a few words.

F1 層【エフワンそう】〔マスコミ・広告業界用語で 20–34 歳の女性の層〕the female 20–34 age group; women in the prime target group for advertising.

M【エム】⇨エス

NG【エヌ・ジー】〔映画・テレビなどで失敗で使えない場面．no good の略〕an outtake; an NG scene; a blooper; a retake;〔不良・無効の意〕bad; failed; rejected.
◇彼はせりふの覚えが悪く **NG** が多い．He doesn't have his lines down so there are a lot of bloopers [NG scenes].
◇電話の音が入り，その場面は **NG** になった．In the middle of things the phone started to ring, so the scene was cut [had to be retaken].
◇**NG** の連発[連続] a string of NG scenes [cuts and retakes]; one NG scene [cut and retake] after another.
◇**NG** を出す〔監督が〕declare a scene [shot] no good [unac-

ceptable]; call for a retake.
◆**NG** 特集〔テレビの〕a (TV) program of bloopers and outtakes [NG scenes].
◆**NG** ワード〔クイズなどで言うと罰になる語句〕a taboo word that, if spoken, invokes a penalty.
◆女優の事務所から **NG** が出てベッドシーンは削除された．The actress's agent complained and had a bedroom scene removed from the final cut.

縁側【えんがわ】
〔カレイやヒラメの〕the (tasty) flesh from around the base of the dorsal and ventral fins of a flounder or flatfish.

援交【えんこう】, 援助交際【えんじょこうさい】
paid [compensated] dating;〔1 回の〕a paid [compensated] date.
◆**援交**する engage in paid [compensated] dating.

炎上【えんじょう】
◆ブログ**炎上**〔ブログの内容に対する批判の書き込みが集中すること〕(blog) flaming; flaming on a blog.
◆人気女優を批判したためにブログが**炎上**してしまった．I got my blog flamed because I dissed a popular actress.

遠恋【えんれん】, 遠距離恋愛【えんきょりれんあい】
a long-distance romance [relationship, love affair]; love across the miles.

お

お熱い【おあつい】 ⇨あつい

追い(出し)コン(パ)【おい(だし)コン(パ)】 a farewell [send-off] party for graduating seniors.

おいしい
◇その給料で週休3日とは**おいしい**話だね．That's a very attractive [appealing] proposition: a high salary like that, and three days a week off as well!

◇**おいしい**話には気をつけなさい．Beware of propositions that are too good to be true.

◇彼は**おいしい**アルバイトを紹介してくれた．He introduced me to a good [high-paying, easy] part-time job.

◇あの男は去年入会して，**おいしい**ところだけを食い荒らしたあげく先月もう退会した．The guy became a member last year, took quick advantage of all the choicest features of membership, then, having done so, quit the club last month.

◇個人が苦労して開発した新製品が儲かると見ると多くの企業が参入して**おいしい**ところをむさぼった．Once they saw that the new product developed through an individual's hard efforts looked as though it would make money, a large number of companies came in and skimmed off the cream.

◇**おいしそうな**女の3人組が僕たちに声をかけてきた．A group of three luscious-looking women called out to us.

お稲荷さん【おいなりさん】〔俗語〕(ball) sack; bag;〔医学用語〕scrotum.

王様ゲーム【おうさまゲーム】

〔飲み会などでくじで「王様」を決め，番号で指名した人をふざけた命令に従わせるゲーム〕a game often played at drinking parties: players draw lots, on one of which the Chinese characters for "king" are written. The other lots are each inscribed with a number. Players call out in one voice, "Who is the King?" And the King responds by requiring his vassals, whom he knows only by a number, to perform a charade or make some other forfeit.

王子様【おうじさま】

a (royal) prince; a prince of the blood (royal).

◇白馬の王子様 a knight on a white horse; a Prince Charming. ★ Prince Charming は「シンデレラ」に登場する王子の名から「理想の男性」を意味する．

◇いつか白馬に乗った王子様が私を迎えに来るはずだ．Someday a Prince Charming riding a white horse is to come to take me away.

◇王子様のような服装で歌い踊る少年5人のグループが今人気だ．A song-and-dance group of five boys who dress up like handsome princes is the rage now.

◇シンデレラは王子様と結婚して幸せに暮らしました．Cinderella married the prince and lived happily ever after.

往復ビンタ【おうふくビンタ】

◇…に往復ビンタを食らわす slap ... in the face forehanded and backhanded; give ... a double slap in the face.

オエ(ー)ッ yuck; yecch; yec.

狼少年【オオカミしょうねん】〔オオカミに育てられた少年〕a wolf child;〔うそばかりつくので信用されなくなった人〕a person who is always crying "Wolf!". ★ cry wolf は「人騒がせなうそをつく」の意で,『イソップ物語』に登場するうそつき少年が「オオカミだ!」と叫んで人をだましたことに由来.
◇あの首相は**狼少年**のようにたびたび「戦後最大の経済危機」を口にしていた. Like a person crying wolf, that prime minister was often using the expression "the biggest postwar economic crisis."
◇どうも私は**狼少年**だと思われているらしい. People seem to think I'm always crying wolf.

大コケ【おおコケ】〔大失敗〕a total [complete] failure; a fiasco; a debacle; a disaster.
◇**大コケ**する be a complete failure;〔口語〕flop; bomb. ★⇨こける

オーバーアクション 〔過剰な演技〕overacting;〔口語〕ham acting. ★ ham は「大根役者(のような臭い芝居をする)」の意.
◇**オーバーアクション**する overact;〔口語〕ham (it up).
◇この場面では**オーバーアクション**にならないように. Be careful not to overact [ham it up] in this scene.

オーバーニー(ソックス),ニーソ 〔ひざより上(の太もも)まであるソックスやストッキング〕overknee [thigh-high] socks [stockings]; overknees; thigh-highs.

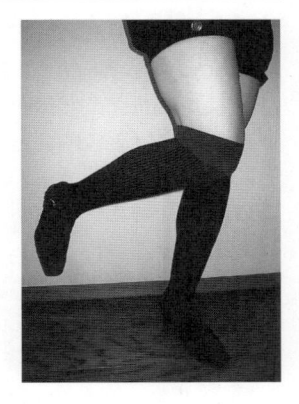

大化け【おおばけ】, 化ける【ばける】

✧**大化け**する, **化ける**〔急に(…に)変わって大成功する〕undergo a metamorphosis [transformation] into ...; metamorphose [turn, be transformed] into a tremendous success; change radically.

✧彼女はさえない女優だったがあの映画で**大化け**した. She wasn't much of an actress until she underwent a total metamorphosis [turned into a megastar] in that film.

✧選挙の結果次第では弱小野党からの**大化け**が期待できる. Depending on the outcome of the election, we could break out of [be transformed from] our present minority-party status.

✧あの選手は海外に移籍して突然**化け**た. He suddenly transformed into a great player after he moved overseas.

✧いやあ, 今年に入って**化け**ましたね. ミリオンセラーですよ. It's amazing! It made a complete turnaround this year and sold a million copies!

オール

〔徹夜(する)〕staying up all night;〔口語〕(pull) an all-nighter.

お母[父]さんっ子【おかあさん[おとうさん]っこ】, お爺[婆]ちゃんっ子【おじいちゃん[おばあちゃん]っこ】
one's mother's [father's, grandad's, gramma's] favorite child; mommy's [daddy's, grandad's, gramma's] pet boy [girl].

おかず ⇨オナペット

お釜【おカマ】
〔ゲイ〕a gay;〔口語〕a queer; a fag; a faggot;〔男娼〕a male prostitute. ★⇨おこげ
◇**おカマを掘る**〔性行為で〕perform [have] anal sex with a man;〔俗語〕bugger a man; give it to a man up [in] the ass.
◇**おカマを掘られる**〔性行為で〕take part in anal sex as the passive partner;〔俗語〕be buggered; take it up the ass;〔車に乗っていて追突される〕be [get] driven into from behind; be plowed into from behind.
◇きのう交差点で**おカマを掘られ**ちゃったよ. Somebody plowed into me from behind at the crossroads yesterday.

お客【お客】
◇〔女性が〕毎月の**お客**さんが来ている〔俗語〕be on the rag. ★ rag は「ぼろ切れ」の意だが,俗語で生理用品のこと.
◇新人の女性は**お客**様扱いされがちだ. Often, rookie women are treated as if they're guests, not regular team members.

億ション【おくション】
a condominium worth (over) a hundred million yen; a hundred-million-yen〔米〕condo [〔英〕flat]; a

superdeluxe condominium.

オケ〔オーケストラの略〕an orchestra; orchestral music. ★⇨カラオケ

お焦げ【おこげ】〔ごはんの〕scorched [burnt] rice; scorched portions of boiled rice; crisp, slightly burned rice (left at the bottom of the pot);〔ゲイと付き合う女性.「おかま」にくっつくことから〕〔俗語〕a fag hag.

おサイフケータイ
　⇨ケータイ

お騒がせ【おさわがせ】
　◇お騒がせ芸能人 an entertainer who is always in the news; an attention-grabbing entertainer.
　◇結局，電源コードが抜けていただけとわかった．とんだお騒がせだった．It just turned out that the plug had been pulled out. It was all a big fuss over nothing. ★⇨チャンチャン

お爺ちゃんっ子【おじいちゃんっこ】⇨おかあさんっこ

おじさん
　⇨おじん

おしまい
　◇それを言っちゃあおしまいよ．That's being too outspoken!; That's some thing that's best left unsaid!
　◇夫婦とはいえ，それを言ったらおしまいだね．There are things even a married couple shouldn't say to each other.

おじょうさん

お嬢さん，お嬢様【おじょうさん［さま］】〔上流家庭の若い女性〕a young lady (of good family);（使用人などが呼びかけて）Miss;〔世間知らずの若い女性〕an innocent [a naive] young girl. ★⇨おひめさま

◇彼女は**お嬢さん**っぽいワンピースがよく似合う．She looks very good in a girlish dress [dresses designed for young girls].

◇この子はいつまでたっても**お嬢さん**で困ったものだ．She still hasn't grown up [out of her childish ways].; This girl is still a spoilt child [young lady].

◇一人娘の彼女は公爵家の**お嬢さん**として大事に育てられた．She had a pampered upbringing as the only daughter of a duke.; As the Duke's only daughter, she received a young lady's sheltered upbringing.

◇**お嬢さん**学校 a school [college] for (rich) young ladies.

◇**お嬢さん**育ちの女性［娘］a woman brought up in a good family; a young woman of good family;〔苦労知らずの〕a woman who has never known hardship;〔わがままな〕a spoiled daughter

◇彼女は**お嬢さん**育ちで，すべてに鷹揚(おうよう)だ．Brought up in a good family, she has a generous approach to [in] all things.

おじん old-timer;〔口語〕oldster;〔口語〕old boy; oldie. ★⇨おば(さ)ん，おやじ

◇**おじん**くさい〔口語〕ancient; antiquated; passé.

おす，おっす〔挨拶語〕a greeting used between close male friends; hi (there)!; hey (man)!

◇「**おっす**」「**おっす**」"Hi (there)!" "Hi(, man)!"

◇**おっす**，おはよっす．Hi! G'morning!; Morning, mate [man]!

押せ押せムード【おせおせムード】being on the offensive;

an attacking mood.

◇後半彼らは**押せ押せムード**となった．They went on the offensive [got into an attacking mood] in the second half.

◇彼の当選で党内は次の選挙に向けて**押せ押せムード**となった．His election put heart into the party [the party in fighting spirit] for the next election.

◇後半同点に持ち込んでからは**押せ押せムード**で試合を進めた．After we got to equalize in the second half, we rode on a wave of confidence for the rest of the game.

◇連勝中のわがチームは**押せ押せムード**だ．After a series of wins our team is in an attacking mood [on the offensive, going all out for victory].

お揃(い)【おそろ(い)】

◇その恋人たちはデートの時にはよく**おそろい**の服で出かける．The two lovers often wear matching clothes when they go out on a date.

◇二人は**おそろい**の帽子をかぶっていた．The two of them were wearing matching caps.

◇**おそろい**のかばんを持っている carry matching briefcases. ★ ⇨ペアルック

お宝グッズ【おたからグッズ】a treasured article. ★⇨アイテム，レア

オタク，オタッキー，ヲタ(ク) an obsessive fan [devotee]; a freak; a junkie.

◇アニメ**オタク** an animation freak.

◇コンピューター**オタク** a computer nerd [geek, weenie].

◇**オタク**族 junkies; freaks. ★⇨あきばけい

落ち研【おちけん】〔落語研究会〕 rakugo club [circle].

おちゃらける 〔茶化す, ふざける〕 make fun of ...; mock; ridicule; laugh ... off [away].
◇おちゃらけた playful; waggish; roguish.

お茶汲み【おちゃくみ】〔茶を淹(い)れること〕(making and) serving tea;〔それをする人〕a person who (makes and) serves tea;〔勤め先でそういう仕事ばかりさせられる女性〕the tea lady.
◇お茶汲みをする (make and) serve tea.
◇お茶汲み仕事 tea pouring; the tea lady's job;〔オフィスでの雑用〕odd jobs around the office.

お茶する【おちゃする】
◇どこかでお茶しない？ Let's stop somewhere for tea.; How about going out for a cup of tea?

落ちる【おちる】〔口説き落とされる〕give in;〔インターネットのチャットなどから抜ける〕leave [quit] (a chat room); go offline;〔原稿執筆が間に合わず雑誌などに掲載できなくなる〕be dropped; be left out.
◇あと一押しで彼女も落ちるに違いない． With a little more nudging I'm sure she'll give in.

追っかけ【おっかけ】〔有名人などを追いかけ回すこと〕following ... around; celebrity chasing;(ストーカー行為) stalking;〔追っかけする人〕a groupie;(ストーカー) a stalker.
◇あの選手はいつもたくさんの追っかけに取り巻かれている． That player [athlete] is always surrounded by a lot of admirers.
◇うちの娘は好きなバンドの追っかけをしている． Our daughter is a groupie of her favorite band.

おっす ⇨おす

お局(様)【おつぼね(さま)】〔仕事場でいばっている古参のOL〕a disparaging term for a middle-aged woman employed as a mid-level manager, whom some of her inferiors compare to a lady-in-waiting at the shogun's palace who is blocking their way to his ear; a senior female worker in a company who supervises in matronly fashion the behavior of junior employees; a matron.

お手付き【おてつき】〔かるた遊びの〕touching a wrong card;〔早押しクイズなどで〕being too quick on the draw;〔主人と関係を結んだ女中〕a mistress.
◇お手付きする touch a wrong card.
◇〔ゲームのルールで〕お手付き3回で失格. If you touch a wrong card three times, you are disqualified.
◇彼女は国王のお手付きとなった. She become the King's [a royal, the royal] mistress.

おでん缶【おでんかん】〔おでんの缶詰〕canned *oden*.

お父さんっ子【おとうさんっこ】 ⇨おかあさんっこ

大人【おとな】
✧**大人**買い〔子供のころ欲しかったが買えなかったものを大人になって存分に買いまくること〕purchasing (of collectibles) by adults.
✧**大人**の味 what appeals to adult taste buds
✧このカレーをベースにさらに香辛料をいろいろ加えれば**大人**の味になります．If you add a few different spices to this curry base you will get a taste that appeals to adults.
✧僕は親の留守中にこっそりワインを飲んでこれが**大人**の味かと思った．Drinking some wine on the sly when my parents weren't home, I thought to myself, "And this is what grown-ups like?"
★⇨おふくろのあじ

オナペット
a person who is *one's* "idol," about whom *one* fantasizes, or whose picture *one* looks at, during masturbation.

鬼【おに】
✧**鬼**買い（おにがい）する〔狂ったように大量に買いまくる〕go on a buying binge [shopping spree].

◇**鬼嫁**(おによめ) a termagant wife; the wife from hell.
◇あの**鬼嫁**は亭主をゴミあつかいだ．The bitch treats her husband like shit. ★⇨あいのむち

オネエ言葉【オネエことば】
◇二，三杯飲むと彼は**オネエ言葉**になりはじめた．After a few cocktails he began talking like a swish.

お婆ちゃんっ子【おばあちゃんっこ】 ⇨おかあさんっこ

お馬鹿(さん)【おばか(さん)】 a silly person; a dope.
◇こんな**おばか**な質問してすみません．Sorry for asking such a silly [ridiculous] question.
◇**おばか**な探偵の珍道中 the adventurous journey of a dopey [goofy, ditzy] detective.
◇これがわからないとしたらよほどの**おばかさん**だ．You're pretty stupid if you don't understand this.
◇健太の**おばかさん**[健太ったら**おばかさん**ねえ]，お母さんがあなたのこと見捨てるはずないじゃない．Don't be silly, Kenta. You don't think I would just leave you, do you?

おば(さ)ん lady; girl;〔口語〕(an) old girl [old maid]. ★⇨おじん
◇私も就職すればあんな**おばん**になるのかなあ．I wonder if I'm going to become an old maid like that, too, when I start working.
◇**おばさん**，じゃまだよ．You're holding up traffic, lady.
◇この服のデザインは**おばさん**くさくて嫌だ．I don't like the design of this dress [these clothes]. It's [they're] for older women.

お姫様【おひめさま】〔育ちがよく世事に疎い女性〕a well-bred woman sheltered from the world; a hothouse plant. ★ ⇨ おじょうさん

✧彼女はお姫様だからなあ，世間のことを何にも知らないよ．Hothouse plant that she is, she knows nothing of the ways of the world.

✧お姫様だっこする[される] carry ... [be carried] in *one's* [...'s] arms.

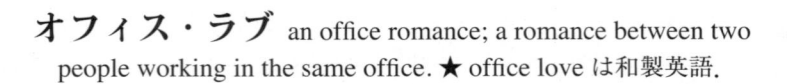

オフィス・ラブ an office romance; a romance between two people working in the same office. ★ office love は和製英語．

オフ会【オフかい】〔ネット上で知り合った者同士が実際に集まって催す会合〕an offline gathering [get-together, party];〔俗語〕face time.

✧オフ会を開催する hold an offline gathering; get together offline.

おふくろの味【おふくろのあじ】

✧この店はおふくろの味を売りものにしている．This restaurant is using "good old home cooking" as its selling point.

(お)坊っちゃん【(お)ぼっちゃん】〔育ちのよい男〕a well-bred young man; an upper-class young man;〔世間知らずの男〕a greenhorn of a young man; a young man innocent of the ways

of the world. ★⇨おじょうさん

◇まるで**お坊ちゃん**だ．〔世間知らずだ〕He is completely innocent (of the ways of the world).; He knows nothing of the world.

◇君のような**おぼっちゃん**にはこれまでの私の苦労はわかるまい．I don't think a well-to-do young man like you can appreciate the hard times I've been through.

◇私はそんな**おぼっちゃん**じゃない．I wasn't born yesterday.; I'm not that green behind the ears.

◇(お)**坊**っちゃん育ち(である) a hothouse plant; have a pampered upbringing.

◇**坊**ちゃん刈り a young boy's close-cropped haircut; a boy's bob; a bowl [mushroom] cut.

◇**坊**ちゃん刈りにする have one's hair cut like a little boy's.

おめでた婚 【おめでたこん】 the wedding of a pregnant bride and her groom. ★⇨できちゃったけっこん

お持ち帰り 【おもちかえり】

◇ここなら**お持ち帰り**用の女がすぐ見つかる．It's a good place to pick someone up to take home.

思われニキビ 【おもわれニキビ】 a pimple, usually a single one on the chin, that some consider the mark of being secretly loved.

お約束【おやくそく】

◇お約束の筋書き a hackneyed [trite, banal] plotline.
◇バナナの皮で滑る**お約束**のギャグ the same tired old gag about slipping on a banana peel.
◇献立は**お約束**のカレーライスだった．The main course was the standard [customary] curry and rice.
◇この連続ドラマはハッピーエンドが**お約束**だ．This drama series always promises a happy ending.

おやじ

◇**おやじ**ギャグ an older man's attempt at humor.
◇変な**おやじ**があとについて来てこわかった．Some creepy old guy followed me and I was really scared.
◇**おやじ**くさいことを言うなよ．Don't talk like an old man.
◇その映画館の観客は**おやじ**ばかりだ．It's a movie theater that attracts mostly middle-aged guys.
◇**おやじ**狩り the mugging of older men (by youth gangs).

おやじギャグの一例
「アルミ缶の上にあるミカン」

親指族【おやゆびぞく】〔携帯電話などを親指で器用に操作する人〕the thumb tribe.

俺【おれ】

◇…と**俺**お前の間柄になる get pally [in] with ...; get on first-name terms with ...
◇彼は社長と**俺**お前の間柄である．He's very pally with the boss.; He's in with the boss.; He and the boss are on first-name terms.

◇人がやるなら俺もというやり方 me-tooism.
◇俺とお前の仲じゃないか．Come on! We're friends [pals], aren't we?
◇俺が俺がの連中 ego-driven men.
◇オレオレ詐欺 an "it's me" scam (in which the caller impersonates a relative in financial distress). ★⇨ふりこめさぎ
◇オレ流 *one's* own (independent) way of thinking [approach].
◇オレ的⇨わたしてき

お笑い【おわらい】

◇えー毎度，ばかばかしいお笑いを一席．Here, let me tell you another [a] crazy story.
◇お笑いタレント a comedian; a comic.
◇お笑い番組 a comedy program.
◇お笑い芸人 a comedian; a comic.
◇若手お笑い芸人 a young comedian [comic].

温度差【おんどさ】

〔物事に対する熱意などの程度の差〕a difference in degrees [the degree] of enthusiasm [interest, commitment, inclination].
◇温度差を感じる sense different degrees of enthusiasm [interest, commitment, inclination].
◇温度差を埋める smooth [cover] over differences in the degree of enthusiasm [interest, commitment, inclination].

オンリーワン

◇ナンバーワンよりもオンリーワンをめざしたい．Rather than just number one, we aim to be the only one.;〔独自性を追求したい〕Our goal is not to be the best—it's to be unique.

か

加圧トレーニング【かあつトレーニング】〔商標〕Kaatu Training.

カード破産【カードはさん】(a) credit-card bankruptcy [insolvency]; (a) bankruptcy caused by excessive credit-card expenditure.

がーん，ガビーン〔驚きを表わす〕
◇「彼，結婚するらしいよ」「がーん！ ショック！」"He's getting married, apparently." "Oh, my God [Oh no]! What a shock!"

外タレ【がいタレ】〔外国人の(テレビ)タレント〕a foreign (TV [media]) personality [celebrity].

買い物依存症【かいものいぞんしょう】compulsive [manic] shopping; a compulsive shopping disorder.
◇買い物依存症の人〔口語〕a shopaholic.

顔出し(パネル)【かおだし(パネル)】〔観光名物やキャラクターを描いて顔の部分に穴を開け，そこから顔を出して写真を撮るパネル〕a free-standing panel painted with a picture of a historical personage, a cartoon character, or the like, with an oval cut out for a person to put his face in and be photographed.

顔ダニ【かおダニ】〔顔面の毛穴などに巣食うニキビダニ〕a (human) demodex mite.

顔パス【かおパス】free admission for being well known.
◇おれは**顔パス**が利く． They'll let me in (at the gate) because they know me [my face].
◇**顔パス**で(入り口・検問などを)通る use *one's* influence to enter [pass]; enter [pass] by using *one's* influence.
◇彼はディスコに**顔パス**で入れた． He was able to go straight into the disco because they recognized him.

顔文字【かおもじ】〔eメールなどで用いる顔マーク〕a smiley; an emoticon.

COLUMN

日英顔文字比較

emoticon は英語の emotion（感情）と icon（アイコン）の合成語．smiley は元来日本で「ピースマーク」や「ニコニコマーク」と呼ばれる丸い笑顔のマークを指す．
日本の顔文字は (^o^) や ヽ(´▽`)/ のように縦向きだが，英語圏の emoticon は次のように左を上にして見る形のものが普通．ただし最近はアニメ風の似顔絵文字や動画などを使うものも多い． ★⇨ ギャル文字

:-)	（笑顔）	:'-(	（泣いている）
:-(	（不機嫌）	:-*	（キスしている）
:-O	（びっくり）	:-}	（ニヤニヤしている）
;-)	（ウィンク）	:-P	（アッカンベー）

カキコ〔インターネットの掲示板などに書き込まれた文章〕a post; a posting; a message.
◇掲示板に**カキコ**する　post a message on a BBS.

ガキの使い【ガキのつかい】, **子供の使い**【こどものつかい】〔要領を得ず,役に立たない使い〕a hopeless [a useless, an incompetent] messenger; a messenger who can't deliver a simple message.
◇〔借金取りなどが〕**ガキの使い**じゃあるまいし,手ぶらで帰るわけにはいかないんだよ．I haven't come all the way here for fun, so don't expect me to leave empty-handed.
◇それじゃまるで**子供の使い**じゃないか．You are just parroting that [what you've been told]!; I want to know your own opinion, not just what you've been told (to tell me). own に強勢を置く．

柿ピー【かきピー】〔「柿の種」あられにピーナッツを混ぜたおつまみ〕a snack-food mixture of spicy rice crackers and peanuts.

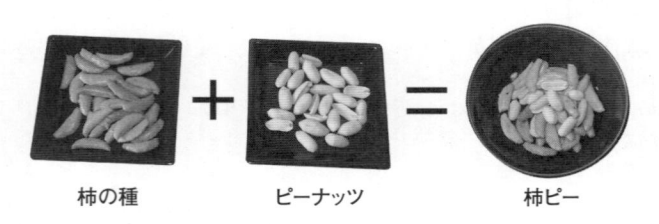

柿の種　＋　ピーナッツ　＝　柿ピー

学園もの【がくえんもの】〔高校生活などを扱ったドラマなど〕a high-school story.

学祭【がくさい】, **学園祭**【がくえんさい】a school [campus] festival.

隠し球【かくしだま】〔野球の〕a hidden-ball trick;〔交渉など

での最後の切り札〕an ace up *one's* sleeve; a trump held back to be played when negotiations threaten to break down.
◆こっちには隠し玉があるんだ．この契約はうちが取ってみせる．I've got an ace up my sleeve and it's going to win that contract for us.
◆彼は二塁打を打ったが隠し球でアウトになった．He hit a double, but was thrown out with the hidden-ball trick.

角栓【かくせん】
〔毛穴の中で皮脂などが固まったもの，コメド〕a comedo ★複数形は comedones.

学ラン【がくラン】
〔詰め襟の学生服〕a student's uniform coat with a stand-up collar;〔学則破りの学生服〕a non-regulation uniform; a student's uniform that bends the regulations of the school dress code.

隠れ…【かくれ…】
〔知られないでいること〕hidden; concealed; secret; unknown; closet; crypto-.
◆隠れキャラ〔テレビゲームなどで裏技を使うと画面に現れるキャラクター〕a hidden [concealed] character.
◆私，ずっとあなたの隠れファンだったんです．I've always been a secret fan of yours.
◆隠れホモ a closet homosexual.

駆けつけ三杯【かけつけさんばい】
forcing a latecomer to drink three cups of sake running.
◆〔遅れて来た人に向かって〕駆けつけ三杯！ As you're late, you must drink three glasses straight off to catch up.

掛け流し【かけながし】
〔温泉で源泉を浴槽に流しっぱなしにしていること〕free-flowing hot-spring water.

ガサ入れ【ガサいれ】〔警察用語で，家宅捜索〕(the carrying out of) a house search;〔口語〕a raid.
◇昨夜，うちの事務所が**ガサ入れ**をくった．Our office got raided last night.

ガシャポン ⇨ ガチャガチャ

ガス抜き【ガスぬき】〔スプレー缶の〕releasing the (remaining) gas;〔不満などの発散〕letting off steam; giving vent to *one's* emotions [frustrations]; calming down; cooling off.
◇双方とも言いたいことを自由に言い合って**ガス抜き**をすることが必要だ．They both need to let off steam by telling each other exactly what's on their minds.
◇最近チームの空気がだいぶ険悪のようだから，ぱーっと騒いで**ガス抜き**でもするか．Things have been going pretty badly for the team, so let's go out on the town and let off a bit of steam.

ガセネタ〔にせの情報〕false information;〔口語〕a bill of goods; a bum steer.
◇あいつに**ガセネタ**をつかまされた．He sold me a bill of goods.; I was given a bum steer. ★ bill of goods は「(偽の)引渡し商品リスト」，bum steer の bum は「浮浪者，怠け者，だめなもの」，steer は「舵を取る」を意味し，合わせて「いい加減な指図」の意．

ガタイがいい〔体つきが大きくてがっしりしている〕well built; husky; big and brawny.

肩叩き【かたたたき】〔凝りをほぐすために肩をたたくこと〕pounding the shoulders (lightly) to relieve stiffness;〔その道具〕a massage device for pounding the back and shoulders;〔退職勧告〕a tap on the shoulder by a superior who is pressuring *one* to

take an early retirement.
◇祖母の**肩叩き**をする (gently) pound the shoulders of *one's* grandmother.
◇**肩たたき**券 a coupon for a free shoulder massage.
◇〔職場で〕**肩叩き**する try to pressure ... into retiring early [(taking) early retirement].
◇**肩叩き**される，**肩叩き**を受ける[にあう] come under pressure to retire early; be pressured into retiring early.

肩出し(ルック)【かただし(ルック)】, 肩見せ(ルック)【かたみせ(ルック)】 off-(the-)shoulder (dress).

ガチ(ンコ) 〔(元来は相撲で)手加減をしない本気のぶつかり合い〕
◇相手がお前の親友であることを忘れろ．**ガチンコ**でやれ．(Don't hold back.) Forget he's [she's] a friend and give it everything you've got.; Forget that your opponent is a friend and be merciless [put your whole heart and soul into the fight].
◇**ガチンコ**勝負[対決] a do-or-die contest; a face-off you put your heart and soul [everything you've got] into;〔真剣勝負〕a game played in earnest; a hotly contested game.

勝ち組【かちぐみ】the victorious group; the winners.
◇産業界の**勝ち組**と負け組 the winners and losers in the manu-

facturing industry.

ガチャガチャ, ガシャポン, ガチャポン
〔玩具入りカプセル自販機〕a capsuled-toy vending machine; a capsule machine.

カチンコ〔撮影の始めと終わりの合図に打つ拍子木〕a clapperboard.

かっくらう, がっつく guzzle *one's* food; wolf down a meal;〔欲が深い〕be greedy for ...
◆みっともないからそんなにがっつくな．It's disgraceful the way you stuff your mouth like that!

学校裏サイト【がっこううらサイト】⇨うら…

合体ロボ(ット)【がったいロボ(ット)】〔アニメなどで〕a combined [combination] robot. ★日本の「変身ロボ」は米国などで Transformer という商品名のおもちゃとして人気があり，特撮映画「トランスフォーマー」にもなっている．ロボットアニメなどの「メカ」は mecha と呼ばれることもある．

がっつく ⇨かっくらう

ガッツポーズ raising *one's* fist(s) in (a show of) triumph.
✧ガッツポーズをする［取る］clench *one's* fist(s)［raise *one's* fist(s), punch the air］in triumph; pump *one's* fist (in the air); give a two-fisted salute.
✧打った瞬間ホームランとわかる当たりで，彼は思わず**ガッツポーズ**をした．The moment he hit the ball he knew it was a homer and he raised his fist in triumph.
✧彼は**ガッツポーズ**をして写真に収まった．The photograph caught him punching the air［with his fist(s) raised］in triumph.

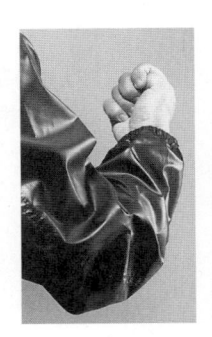

ガッツリ〔たっぷり，十分に〕
✧**ガッツリ**食べる have a bellyful; eat *one's* fill.

勝手サイト【かってサイト】〔NTT ドコモの i モードサービスで閲覧可能なウェブサイトのうちの非公式サイト〕an *i-mode* (Web) site not officially sponsored by NTT; a voluntary site

カップラーメン，カップ麺【カップめん】instant noodles in a (Styrofoam) cup; "cup noodles."

カップルつなぎ lovers holding hands with fingers interlaced / holding hands in the lovers' clasp.

ガッポガッポ，がっぽり

✧ガッポガッポ(と)金が入ってくる oodles and oodles of money come in; money rolls in. ★英語ではレジの入金時に鳴る音を使って ka-ching! と表わすことがある．

✧がっぽりもうける make oodles [oodles and oodles, wads].

✧彼は競馬でがっぽりもうけた．He made oodles [wads, piles, loads] of money on the (horse) races.

✧いくら働いても税金でがっぽり取られるからむなしいよ．It breaks your heart when no matter how hard you work they take away a pile in taxes.

家庭内【かていない】

✧家庭内別居 living apart under the same roof.

✧家庭内暴力 domestic violence（略：DV）; violence in the home.

✧家庭内離婚 being divorced but still living together; living apart under the same roof; in-home separation. ★⇨かめんふうふ

ガテン系【ガテンけい】〔肉体労働・現業職．主に現業職

を扱う就職雑誌『ガテン』より〕"Gaten"-type work; manual labor of the kind advertised [the sort of job they advertise] in the magazine "Gaten"; 〔ガテン系の人〕a "Gaten"-type worker; a manual laborer.

カニかま(ぼこ) steamed fish paste shaped and colored to resemble crab meat; imitation crab sticks.

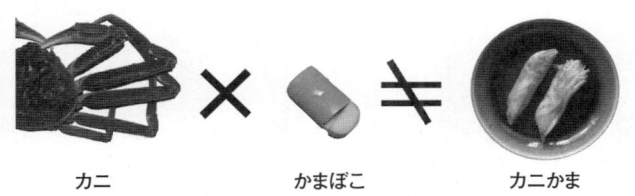

カニ　　　かまぼこ　　　カニかま

彼女【かのじょ】〔恋人〕a girlfriend; a sweetheart;〔口語〕a steady; *one's* girl. ★⇨かれし, いまカノ, もとカノ
◇〔呼びかけて〕ちょっと，そこの**彼女**！ Hey you [young lady, Miss].; Excuse me, Miss.
◇息子に**彼女**ができた．My son has got [found] a girlfriend.
◇僕の**彼女**になってくれ．Be [Do be] my girlfriend.
◇**彼女**はまだいないのか．Don't you have a girlfriend yet?; You still don't have a girlfriend?
◇彼氏[**彼女**]いない歴5年です．I've had no boyfriend [girlfriend] for five years.; I've gone five years without a boyfriend [girlfriend].

下半身【かはんしん】〔遠回しに，性器〕the [*one's*] private parts; *one's* privates; the [*one's*] genitals.
◇日本のマスコミは政治家の**下半身**に甘かった．The Japanese media used to leave a politician's sex life alone [didn't used to deal with the sexual goings-on of politicians].
◇**下半身**には人格はないという人もいる．Some claim that we are all the same below the waist [character is irrelevant when it

comes to sex].
◇あの雑誌は**下半身**のことばかり取り上げる．That magazine only deals in sex and scandal [panders only to the lowest instincts].
◇…の前で**下半身**を露出する expose oneself; flash *one's* penis [privates, 〔口語〕willy] at [in front of] ...; flash *oneself*.
◇**下半身**スキャンダル (a) sex [sexual] scandal.
◇**下半身**デブだ．have a fat bottom and legs; be pear-shaped.

ガビーン　⇨がーん

被り物【かぶりもの】〔仮装用の〕a headpiece. ★⇨きぐるみ
◇馬の**かぶりもの** a horse headpiece; a horse-head stage prop.

牛のかぶりもの

カブる〔重複する〕
◇ネタが**かぶる** tell joke after joke with similar punch lines that draw less and less laughter; do the same sort of comedy routine to poorer and poorer effect.

噛ませ犬【かませいぬ】a straw man; a fall guy; a patsy.

カミングアウト〔自分が同性愛者であると公表すること〕a coming-out.

◇カミングアウトする come out as gay or lesbian.

噛む【かむ】〔とちる〕fumble.
◇せりふを噛む muff *one's* lines;〔俗語〕fluff.

カメラ目線【カメラめせん】looking [speaking, facing] into the camera. ★⇨うえからめせん

仮面夫婦【かめんふうふ】a couple who only go through the motions of being husband and wife. ★⇨かていない

鴨【カモ】〔だましやすい相手〕〔口語〕a pigeon; a gull; a sitting duck; a fall guy; a pushover; an easy [a soft, a good] mark; a sucker; a patsy.
◇カモが葱(ねぎ)を背負って来る，カモねぎだ (a case of) a duck bringing along other ingredient for a hot pot;〔だまされやすい人が自分の方から近づいてくること〕(a case of) a sucker coming along just at an opportune time;〔好都合の上にも好都合である〕(this's) doubly convenient; be in double luck; something so good one couldn't ask for anything better; a double stroke of good luck.
◇カモネギみたいなそんなうまい話があるものか．だまされるなよ．It's too good to be true. Don't get taken in.

◇いい**カモ**が来た．やつに売りつけよう．Here's an easy mark. Let's sell it to him.
◇…を**カモ**にする，**カモ**る make a sucker out of . . . ; dupe;〔口語〕take in; take . . . for a ride; pull a fast one (on . . .); put one over (on . . .).
◇**カモ**にされる be taken in; be duped;〔口語〕be taken for a ride.

通い妻【**かよいづま**】〔普段は同居せず時々夫の元へ通って世話をする妻，また時折恋人の家へ通う女性〕a wife or lover who lives separately but regularly visits her husband or lover.

カラオケ〔カラオケで歌うこと〕karaoke ★ほぼ英語化しており，発音は「キャラオーケイ」に近い; singing along with karaoke music; singing to the accompaniment of a karaoke machine;〔器楽伴奏だけの録音〕a pre-recorded backing (tape [CD]); the prerecorded accompaniment to a song.
◇**カラオケ**に合わせて歌う sing along with [to] karaoke music; sing (a song) to the accompaniment of a karaoke machine.
◇私の趣味は**カラオケ**です．One of the things I like to do is to sing at karaoke bars.
◇大広間には**カラオケ**があります．ご自由にお使いください．Please feel free to use the karaoke (machine) in the saloon.
◇二次会は**カラオケ**に行こう．Let's go on to a karaoke place (to follow up the party).
◇最新の歌もかなり古い歌も**カラオケ**に入っている．We now have karaoke (versions) for both the latest songs and quite old ones.
◇**カラオケ**酒場 a karaoke [sing-along] pub.
◇**カラオケ**・セット a karaoke machine [set]; a sing-along tape

player unit.
✧**カラオケ大会**〔祭りなどの〕a karaoke contest [competition].
✧**カラオケバー** a karaoke [sing-along] bar.
✧**カラオケハウス，カラオケボックス，カラオケルーム** a karaoke joint;〔個室〕a karaoke booth [room, cubicle].

カラコン，カラー・コンタクト（レンズ） a colored [tinted] contact lens.

カラスの足跡【からすのあしあと】〔目じりの小じわ〕crow-feet, crow's-feet.

空伝(票)【からでん(ぴょう)】a fictious receipt.

ガラポン〔回転式の抽選器〕a lottery wheel.

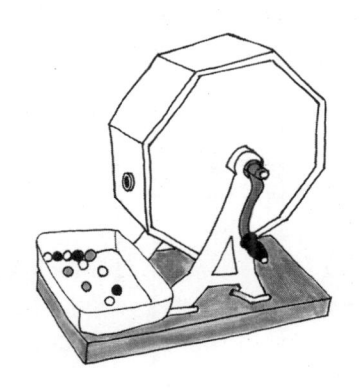

空メール【からメール】〔応募などでメールアドレスを伝えるために送る，内容がブランクのメール〕(a) blank mail.

カリスマ
◇カリスマ美容師[モデル，主婦，バイヤー，シェフ，教師] a charismatic hairdresser [fashion model, homemaker, buyer, chef, teacher].

加齢臭【かれいしゅう】 the smell of an aged person.

彼(氏)【カレ(シ)】〔恋人〕a boyfriend; a steady. ★⇨いまカレ，もとカレ，ゲット
◇娘が**彼氏**を連れてきた．My daughter brought her present young man.
◇あの男が君の**彼氏**か．So that's your boyfriend?
◇**彼氏**いない歴 ⇨かのじょ

枯れ専【かれせん】〔20–30歳年上の"枯れた"男性に魅力を感じる女性〕a (younger) women who prefers older men [likes her men (to be) older]; a daddy-snatcher.

川の字【かわのじ】
◇わが家では親子3人**川の字**になって寝ている．We three sleep together, with our child between us.

ガングロ，がん黒 a cosmetic vogue for a deeply tanned face, white eyeliner, and false eyelashes.
◇ガングロの女の子 a girl with a face made up to look black.

完結【かんけつ】
◇一話**完結**のドラマ a TV drama series with self-contained episodes.
◇十話[十回]**完結**のドラマ a TV drama series with ten episodes [with a ten-episode story arc].

完食【かんしょく】 eating ... completely;〔口語〕eating every last scrap (of a meal).
◇**完食**する finish eating (a huge portion of food);〔口語〕eat every last scrap (on *one's* plate).

缶チューハイ【かんチューハイ】 (a) canned *shochu* cocktail; a can of *shochu* mixed with soda water or soda pop.

缶バッジ【かんバッジ】〔通例ブリキ製で円盤型のバッジ〕a tin badge.

岩盤浴【がんばんよく】 "bedrock bathing"; a "bedrock bath"; a health and beauty treatment in which people lie on heated rock slabs.

カンペ〔テレビなどで台詞や指示を書いて画面外で出演者に見せるボード〕idiot board;〔試験中のカンニングペーパー〕a cheat sheet: a crib (sheet [note]); a pony.

ガン見する【ガンみする】〔じろじろ見る〕stare; glare; look up and down.

ガンをつける[とばす] 〔やくざなどが〕 stare at [fasten *one's* eyes on] ... (with sinister motives)

✧人相のよくない男に「ガンをつけたな」とからまれた. A man with a nasty look said I'd been staring at him, and he tried to pick a fight.

✧2つのグループは互いに鋭いガンをとばしあった. The two gangs eyed each other fiercely.

き

きー(っ) 〔悲鳴・ブレーキ音〕a screech;〔こすれる音〕a squeak; a squeal.
◇きーっ, 悔しい！ Damn! The dirty [lousy] so-and-so!

キーマカレー 〔インド起源の挽き肉カレー〕keema curry.

スリランカのキーマカレー

期間限定(商)品【きかんげんてい(しょう)ひん】 a product [an item] on sale for a limited time [period] (only).

ギクッ 〔驚く様子〕a start; a fright; alarm.
◇ぎくっとする start; take fright; be alarmed.
◇「家で練習してきたかどうか，先生にはすぐわかる．さあ，暗唱してごらん．」「ぎくっ」 "I'll be able to tell, right away, whether you practiced at home or not. Okay, let me hear you recite it from memory." "Gulp!"

着ぐるみ【きぐるみ】
◇ゴリラ[怪獣]の着ぐるみを着た男 a man in a gorilla [monster]

suit. ★⇨かぶりもの，コスプレ

キショい ⇨キモい

騎乗位【きじょうい】〔性交体位の〕the straddling position.

傷物にする【きずものにする】
◇娘を**傷物**にされて父親は激怒した．Her father was furious when his daughter lost her virginity.

キセル 〔不正乗車〕cheating on train [bus] fares.
◇**キセル**乗車する pay only for the first and last segments of a rail ride; steal a ride on a train without paying for the middle part of the journey.
◇**キセル**をやってつかまる get caught trying to cop a free ride (on the train).

…キター！ That's it!!!!!; I've got it!!!!!
◇「あんな女簡単に落として見せるぜ」「おーっとモテ男くん**キター**！」"I'll get her in a snap" "Here he comes: Mr. smooth operator."
◇ばんざい金曜日**キター**！ Yippee! It's Friday!

帰宅部【きたくぶ】〔放課後すぐ帰宅してしまいクラブ活動をしないこと〕a "going-straight-home" club.
◇あいつは**帰宅部**だから，3時以降は学校にいないよ．The only activity that interests him is going home [He's the sort with no outside interests], so he's never in school after three.

機変【きへん】〔携帯電話の機種変更〕a model change.

◇**機変**する change the model (of *one's* mobile phone);〔口語〕get a new (type of) mobile phone.

決まる【きまる】, 決める【きめる】

〔さまになる〕look good [stylish,〔口語〕sharp];〔型どおり整える〕dress formally; dress up;〔口語〕dress to kill [to the nines].

◇その日の彼女はブランド物のスーツで**決めて**いた．On that day she was dressed to kill in a brand-name suit. ◇今日はタキシードでビシッと**決めて**行くぞ．Today I'm going to go looking smart in a tuxedo. ◇そのスーツ，**決まって**いるね．That suit looks really good on you. ◇彼がギターを弾く姿はなかなか**決まって**いる．When he's playing the guitar he looks sharp. ◇けさは髪型がなかなかうまく**決まらなかった**．This morning my hairdo just wouldn't stay in place. ◇ポーズが**決まる**，ポーズを**決める** strike a pose and hold it. ★⇨きめぜりふ

決め台詞【きめぜりふ】

a closing pitch [spiel]; a killer [surefire] line.

キモい，キショい

〔気持ち悪い，気色悪いを縮めた俗語〕yucky; gross. ◇…が**キモい** be grossed out by ….

客【きゃく】

◇**客**いじり〔芸人が観客に話しかけて笑いを取ろうとすること〕playing to the audience. ★⇨おきゃく，パンダ

逆切れ，逆ギレ【ぎゃくぎれ】

a counterblast; a counteroffensive; (a) backlash. ★⇨きれる

◇…に**逆ギレ**する snap back at ….

◇メーカーに電話で苦情を言ったら**逆切れ**した担当者に罵倒された．When I called the manufacturer to register a complaint, the person in charge turned the tables and bawled *me* out.

逆玉(の輿)【ぎゃくたま(のこし)】 a man marrying into wealth.
◇彼は逆玉を狙っている．He's a fortune hunter looking to marry into money [for a wealthy woman to marry, for a free ride].

逆ナン【ぎゃくナン】〔女性が男性をナンパすること〕a man being approached by a woman (and asked for a date);〔口語〕picking up a guy.

キャバクラ a cabaret club; a bar with female companions for male customers.

キャピキャピ
◇キャピキャピの女の子 skylarking [frolicking, frisky] girls.

キャラ(クター)〔個性・性格・登場人物〕character. ★⇨かくれ…，いじられキャラ，ごとうちキャラ，だつりょく，ゆるキャラ
◇キャラクターグッズ[商品] character goods [merchandise]; products featuring cartoon characters.
◇ユニークなキャラ(クター)を売り物にする capitalize on *one's* unique character.
◇アニメ[漫画]のキャラ a character in a cartoon [comic].
◇彼女はキャラが濃すぎて友人が少ない．She's so intense by nature that she has few friends.
◇主人公から脇役に至るまでキャラ立ちまくりの映画だ．From the lead to the supporting roles it's a film chockfull of unforgettable oddball characters.

ギャラ泥棒【ギャラどろぼう】⇨すうじ，きゅうりょうどろぼう

ギャル〔女の子〕〔俗語〕a gal. ★⇨えーぶい，こギャル

◇**ピチピチギャル** a girl in the bloom of youth.

◇**ギャル系**（ファッション）"gal-type" fashion; describing a fashion adopted by young Japanese teenage girls, characterised by dyed hair, dark sunburnt skin and flashily matched clothing.

◇**ギャル文字** "gal characters"; a writing system using unconventional kanji and symbols in place of similar-looking standard characters.

COLUMN

英語版ギャル文字？

英語にもギャル文字に似た「リートスピーク，リート語 (leet(speak))」と呼ばれる，文字を形の似た他の数字や記号に置き換えたり，わざとつづりを違えたりするネットやメール上の隠語表記がある．leet は元来コンピューターの「くろうと」を指す elite から来たもの．2ちゃんねるなどの「史ね(＝死ね)」「厨房(＝中坊；中学生並みの幼稚な坊主)」といった言葉遣いにも似ている．

リートスピークにはたとえば次のような書き方がある．

A → @ , 4	J → | (縦棒)	T → 7
B → 8, I3	K → |(, |<, x	U → |_|
C → (	L → 1, | (縦棒)	V → \\/
D → I)	M → /\\/\\	W → \\/\\/
E → 3	N → /\\/	X → ><
F → |=	O → 0 (ゼロ)	Y → '/
G → 9, 6	P → |*	Z → 2
H → |-|	R → I2	
I → 1, | (縦棒)	S → 5, $	

これに従って例えば leetspeak → 1337$p34I(のようになる．他に teh (the)，pwn (own「(ゲームなどで)やっつける，ボコボコにする」)，pr0n (porn「ポルノ，エロ」)，joo (you)，n00b (noob, newbie「しろうと」) などのつづり変えもある．

ギャルゲー a (video) game featuring young girls.

キャンギャル，キャンペーンガール a sales-convention [sales-campaign, trade-show] mascot girl. ★⇨コンパニオン

休肝日【きゅうかんび】〔酒を飲まない日〕a teetotal day; a day off (the) drink.
◇少なくとも週に2日は休肝日をもうけるようにと医者に言われた．I was told by my doctor to make two days a week teetotal days [take two days off the drink a week].

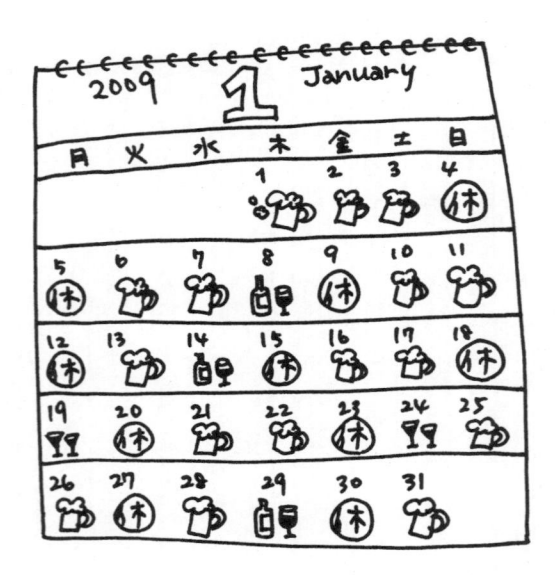

給料泥棒【きゅうりょうどろぼう】a parasite; a freeloader; a shirker; a slacker; a worker who does not deserve his salary.

局アナ【きょくアナ】〔放送局に勤務するアナウンサー〕a career TV [radio] announcer.

巨乳【きょにゅう】big [full] breasts; an ample [a big] bosom.

きり番【きりばん】〔きりのいい番号〕a round number (of Web page hits).
◇そのホームページを訪れたとき，カウンターが**きり番**だったのでうれしくなった．I was really happy because the page counter was at a round number when I accessed that Web site.

義理チョコ【ぎりチョコ】social courtesy [obligatory] chocolates; chocolates that one feels oblige to give;〔口語〕just-to-be-nice chocolates. ★⇨ほんめい，ともチョコ

切れる【キレる】〔冷静さを失う〕lose *one's* composure; get worked up; lose control;〔俗語〕lose *one's* cool;（かっとなる）snap; explode;〔口語〕fly off the handle; blow up; blow *one's* top;〔俗語〕lose it.
◇就職しろと親父がいつまでもうるさく言うので**キレて**しまった．I snapped [flew off the handle] when my father wouldn't quit hounding me about getting a job.
◇あいつは**キレたら**何をするかわからない．You just don't know what he might do if he loses control (of himself).
◇そのとき私は**キレ**そうだった．I almost lost control then.
◇おれは**キレた**ぞ．I've just about had enough.; I've had (just about) all I can take.; That does it!; That's it!

キンキラ(キン), ギンギラ(ギン)

◇キンキラキンに着飾る wear showy clothes; be dressed up to the nines.

◇ギンギラ(ギン)の(アクセサリー) over-bright and shiny (accessories); gaudy; flashy; showy. ★ヒップホップ系の俗語では派手な宝石類のアクセサリーを bling-bling と呼ぶ.

ギンギン

◇ギンギンに踊りまくる dance ecstatically.

金太郎飴【きんたろうあめ】

◇どこを切っても金太郎飴のような無味乾燥なレポートだ. It's a cut-and-dried report that hasn't a single insight to offer.

◇ここの社員はまるで金太郎飴だ. At this company you can't tell one manager from another: they're all cut from the same pattern.

く

空気【くうき】〔雰囲気, 状況〕an atmosphere.
◇職場の**空気** the atmosphere [spirit] of a workplace.
◇場の**空気**を読む catch [sense] the mood [feeling]; take a [the] hint.
◇あの子は**空気**が読めない[KY だ]から嫌われている．She never knows what's going on around her [can't read what's in the wind]. So people find her difficult to deal with.

クールビズ〔ノーネクタイの夏のビジネスウェア〕"cool-biz menswear"; no-necktie men's summer office wear.

ググる〔検索エンジン Google でネット検索する〕Google. ★動詞として使う．
◇そんなことは**ググ**ればすぐわかる．Do a Google search [Just Google it] and you'll find it right away.
◇その言葉を**ググ**ってみたが，1件もヒットしなかった．I Googled the word, but didn't get a single hit.; A Google search didn't give me [produce, turn up] a single hit.

臭い【クサい】〔わざとらしい〕unskilled; clumsy; hammy.
◇**クサい**演技だなあ．It's a pretty clumsy performance.

糞【くそ】〔大便〕〔俗語〕crap;〔卑語〕shit;〔ののしる時や奮起する時に使う言葉〕〔俗語〕crap;〔卑語〕shit;〔卑語〕a turd.
◇くそをする defecate;〔俗語〕(have a) crap;〔卑語〕(have a) shit].
◇(ええ)くそっ！ Damn (it)!; Blast (it)!; Hell!; Heck!; Shit!

✧くそっ，負けてたまるか．Damn it, I'm not going to let that guy beat me!
✧あのくそおやじめ．That damn [bloody] old fool!
✧民主主義なんてくそ食らえだ．To hell with democracy!; Democracy be blowed [damned]!; 〔俗語〕Democracy sucks!
✧「今日コンパなんですけど」「この忙しいさなかにコンパもくそもあるか」"I'm supposed to go to a party tonight...." "A party when we're so busy?? You gotta be kidding!"
✧このくそ忙しいときに！ Just when I'm so damn [〔卑語〕fucking] busy!

クソゲー
〔糞のようにつまらないゲーム〕shitty video game; megaboring video game.

グダグダ
✧グダグダ文句ばかり言う complain on and on, tediously.
✧グダグダする loaf; lie around doing nothing.
✧暑い日はいつも家でグダグダしている．On hot days I just lie around the house.

口裂け女【くちさけおんな】
〔都市伝説の，口が耳まで裂けた怪女〕a supernatural woman with her mouth sliced open from ear to ear.

口パク【くちパク】
〔録音した音に合わせて口を動かすこと〕lip-sync(h); lip-sync(h)ing. ★唇 (lip) を音に合わせてシンクロ (synchronize) させることから．
✧「イエスタデイ」を口パクで歌う lip-sync(h) (to) *Yesterday*.

食っちゃ寝【くっちゃね】
✧冬休みに食っちゃ寝していたらすっかり太ってしまった．I ate

and slept my way through the winter holidays and put on a lot of weight. ★⇨しょうがつぶとり, ふゆぶとり

くっちゃべる ⇨ダベる

グラサン 〔サングラス〕(a pair of) sunglasses;〔口語〕shades.

クラシックパンツ 〔ふんどし〕a loincloth; a breechcloth; a breechclout; a G-string (for men).

グラビア a photogravure; a gravure.
◇雑誌のグラビア a magazine photogravure.
◇グラビアアイドル, グラドル pinup [poster] girl [idol]; gravure idol.

クリアする
◇新しいテレビゲームを買ったが, 最初の画面がなかなかクリアできないでいる. I bought a new TV game, but I'm having trouble clearing [getting past] the first screen [stage].

クリオネ 〔ハダカカメガイ科の軟体動物の通称. 学名 *Clione limacina*〕a (naked) sea butterfly; a sea angel.

グルーピー　a groupie. ★⇨おっかけ

グルメ　〔美食家・食通〕a gourmet; a food buff; a fine food lover.
◇グルメ志向 an interest in [a preference for] fine food.
◇グルメ情報 fine food lovers' information; a guide to good eating.
◇グルメ番組[雑誌, 本] a program [magazine, book] for fine food lovers.
◇グルメブーム a gourmet [fine food] boom.

クレーマー　〔企業に執拗に苦情を申し立てる客〕a customer who makes extremely unjust and persistent complaints about a commercial product. ★「クレームをつける」は complain または make a complaint と言い, この意味で claim は使わない.

ぐれる　〔堕落する〕go astray; stray from the right path; turn bad; go wrong [amiss].
◇ぐれた息子 a prodigal son; a delinquent son.
◇彼は希望の学校に入れず, ぐれだした. When he couldn't get into the school he wanted, he began to go astray.
◇学業半ばにぐれてしまった. He fell into evil ways partway through his studies.

クローザー　〔抑え投手〕a closer.

黒毛和牛【くろげわぎゅう】, 黒毛和種【くろげわしゅ】
a breed of cattle with black hair produced by crossbreeding Japanese and non-Japanese stock.

黒服【くろふく】〔風俗店などの従業員・客引きの男性〕a male staff member of a sex establishment (often seen in black clothes); a pimp.

け

傾向と対策【けいこうとたいさく】
◇入試の傾向と対策 trends in entrance exams and how to deal with them; strategies for recent exams.

芸細【げいこま】, 芸が細かい【げいがこまかい】
be attentive to (the) details; artful; subtle;〔悪知恵に長けた〕cunning; foxy;〔凝った〕elaborate; refined; sophisticated; ornate; recherché; soigné;〔凝りすぎの〕fussy.
◇ほう, 名刺に自筆の似顔絵を入れるとは芸が細かい. Now isn't that clever [a clever touch]! A visiting card with your self-portrait on it!

掲示板【けいじばん】
〔ネットワーク上の電子掲示板〕an electronic bulletin board; a bulletin board system; a BBS.
◇掲示板にメッセージを書き込む post a message on a bulletin board. ★⇨カキコ
◇掲示板管理人[管理者] a bulletin board manager.
◇掲示板サイト a bulletin board site.

携帯(電話)【けいたい(でんわ)】⇨ケータイ

芸人【げいにん】
an entertainer; a performer; an artiste;〔集合的に〕talent;〔多芸の人〕a multitalented person; a person with multiple talents.
◇二人組の芸人 a (performing) duo.
◇バラエティー番組の芸人を集める recruit talent for a variety show.

◇あの男はなかなかの**芸人**だ．He is quite an entertainer [a performer].
◇**芸人**根性 the performing spirit; showmanship.
◇**芸人**仲間 (people in) show business; the performing fraternity.
★⇨おわらい

ケーキバイキング 〔ケーキの食べ放題〕an all-you-can-eat cake buffet.

ゲーセン，ゲームセンター a game [video] arcade; a game center; an amusement arcade.
◇**ゲームセンター**で遊ぶ spend time in a game arcade.
◇**ゲームセンター**に入り浸る hang out at a game arcade.

ケータイ，携帯(電話)【けいたい(でんわ)】a cellular phone; a cellphone; a mobile [portable, pocket] phone. ★ mobile phone または a moble は主に英国で使われる．⇨きへん
◇彼の**ケータイ**にかける call him on his cellular phone.
◇…の**ケータイ**にメッセージを入れておく leave a message on …'s cellular phone.
◇**ケータイ**の着信音 the (call) sound of a cellular phone. ★⇨ちゃくメロ
◇**ケータイ**の電源を切る turn off *one's* cellular phone.
◇**ケータイ**をマナーモードにする，**ケータイ**が圏外だ⇨マナーモード，けんがい ★信号の強さを示す「アンテナ」は普通 bar と呼ばれる．⇨バリさん
◇〔電車内のアナウンスで〕車内での**携帯電話**のご使用は，他のお客さまの迷惑になりますのでおやめください．To avoid annoying the other passengers, please do not use your cellular phone.; For the comfort and convenience of others, passengers are requested not to use cellular phones in this car.

◇デジタル方式の**携帯電話** a digital cellular phone.
◇ハンドフリーの**携帯電話** a hands-free cellular phone
◇プリペイド方式の**携帯電話** a prepaid cellular phone.
◇**携帯電話会社** a mobile [cellular] phone operator.
◇**携帯発固定着料金** a rate for calls from mobile to fixed phones.
◇**ケータイ通販** online shopping by cellphone [mobile phone].
◇**ケータイ読書** reading (books) on a cellphone [mobile phone].
◇**ケータイ小説** a cellphone [mobile-phone] novel.
◇**ケータイゲーム** a mobile (phone) game.
◇**ケータイ**(用)サイト a cellphone [cellular, mobile-phone] (Web) site. ★⇨かってサイト
◇**ケータイ用ストラップ** a cellphone [mobile-phone] strap.
◇**ケータイ用充電器** a cellphone [mobile-phone] battery charger. ★⇨じゅうでん
◇カメラ付き**ケータイ** a camera (cellular [mobile]) phone; a (cell) phone cam. ★⇨しゃメ
◇**ケータイメール**〔メールによる通信〕cell [mobile] phone e-mail;〔1通のメール〕a cell [mobile] phone e-mail (message). ★英米では携帯を使う文字通信をしばしば text (message) あるいは SMS と呼ぶ. ⇨メール
◇おサイフ**ケータイ**〔NTT ドコモの提供する, 携帯電話を財布代わりに使える電子マネーサービスの商標〕an "O-saifu Keitai"; a wallet cell phone; a mobile wallet.
◇**ケータイ依存症**[中毒] (a) cellphone [mobile (phone)] addiction; (an) addiction to cellphones [mobile phones]; phonaholism; (cell)phone addiction;〔ケータイが手放せない人〕a phonaholic; a (cell)phone addict.
◇**携帯ゲーム機** a portable (video) game console [machine].
◇**携帯**(音楽)プレーヤー a portable music player.
◇**携帯トイレ**[灰皿] a portable toilet [ashtray].
◇**携帯ナビゲーション**〔GPS 機能搭載の携帯機器によって歩行

者を誘導すること〕portable navigation.
◇**携帯**ナビゲーション機器［システム］a portable navigation device [system].

KY【ケーワイ】〔「空気が読めない」の頭文字〕⇨くうき

激…【げき…】〔強調の接頭辞〕extremely; terrifically;〔口語〕super. ★⇨ちょう…, ど…, なえ, レア
◇**激**旨(うま)の店 a super-delicious restaurant.
◇**激**辛(から)の(カレー) fiery hot [super-spicy, extra-spicy] (curry).
◇**激**辛食品 super-spicy food.
◇**激**辛ブーム a boom [fad] for super-spicy food.
◇**激**安商品 dirt-cheap goods.
◇**激**安店［ショップ］a super discounter.
◇…を**激**写する take a powerful [intense] photo(graph) of ….
◇**激**太り extreme weight gain;〔口語〕ballooning up.
◇**激**やせ extreme thinning [weight loss].
◇**激**やせする lose a great deal of weight.
◇彼女は拒食症になって**激**やせした．She got anorexia and became rail thin.

ゲジゲジ眉【ゲジゲジまゆ】a pair of thick eyebrows.

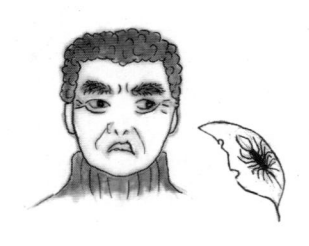

ケチョンケチョン　thoroughly; utterly.

◇けちょんけちょんにやりこめられる get [be given] a good telling-off; catch it good and proper; catch [be given] hell.

◇彼の新刊小説は書評でけちょんけちょんにけなされてしまった．His new novel got a totally scathing review [was lambasted].

◇「試合どうだった？」「もうけちょんけちょん」"How was the game.?" "We were thrashed.; They beat us hollow.; They wiped the floor with us."

ケツ〔俗語〕the backside; the bum; the ass; the fanny; the butt; the arse.

◇ケツの穴 the anus; the back passage;〔卑語〕the asshole.

◇ケツの穴の小さい miserly; narrow-minded; chickenhearted; timid; cowardly.

◇なんてケツの穴の小さいやつだ．How narrow-minded you are!

◇ケツの穴の小さいことを言うな．Don't be so narrow-minded!

◇ケツの青い(若造) (a young person) wet behind the ears.

◇ケツをまくる〔(追いつめられて)攻撃的になる〕suddenly turn aggressive (when cornered); take the offensive;〔(居直って)威嚇する〕become overbearing; put on airs; get on *one's* high horse;〔自暴自棄になる〕throw everything aside; throw caution to the winds.

◇ケツバット (a) spanking with a baseball bat. ★⇨ケツカッチン

結果オーライ【けっかオーライ】

◇いろいろ問題はあっても，結果オーライならいいじゃないか．There may be various problems, but surely that's fine as long as things work out all right in the end.

ケツカッチン　〔予定時間帯の最後が次の予定時間帯と

ぶつかっているため，前の仕事の終わり時間が決められてしまうさま〕a fixed ending time [deadline].

月給泥棒【げっきゅうどろぼう】 ⇨きゅうりょうどろぼう

月9【げっく，げつく】 *Gekku*, *Getsuku* (Monday at Nine); pet name and time slot of drama series broadcast on Fuji-TV Network. Usually targeting young women, since the 1990s the dramas have been, by consensus, the most successful and marketable on network TV.

ゲット(する) 〔ものにする〕get; obtain; win.
✧合コンで彼氏を**ゲットする** find a boyfriend [hook up with a boy] at a mixed party.
✧早食い競争で賞金を**ゲットした**．I won the prize offered at a speed-eating contest.
✧この女性は宝くじで見事100万円を**ゲット**！ She won a million yen in the lottery!

月曜病【げつようびょう】 Monday disease; not wanting to go back to work after the weekend; horror at the prospect of Monday morning.

ケバい
✧**ケバい**服装[化粧] glitzy clothes [makeup].
✧彼女最近**ケバく**なってきた．She's turned glitzy recently.

げほげほ 〔せきの音〕(the sound of) a wet cough [wet coughing].
✧先月から風邪をひきっぱなしで，**げほげほ**(と)せきをし続けている．I've had a cold with a wet cough ever since last month.

ゲロする〔嘔吐する〕vomit; throw up;〔白状する〕confess (the truth);〔犯人が〕own up to a crime.

ゲロ袋【ゲロぶくろ】⇨エチケットぶくろ

圏外【けんがい】
◇(携帯電話が)圏外である be out of (service) range; have no reception [signal].
◇この地下街は(電波の)圏外だ.〔携帯電話の電波が届かない〕This underground arcade is outside cellphone service range.
◇圏外〔携帯電話の表示〕No Service. ★⇨ケータイ, バリさん

原チャリ【げんチャリ】〔原動機付き自転車〕a bicycle with a motor attached; a motorized [motor] bicycle; a motorbike; a moped;〔法律上の分類で〕a motorized bicycle [motorcycle] with a displacement of less than 50cc.

限定商品【げんていしょうひん】⇨きかんげんていひん, ごとうちキャラ

現生【げんなま】〔現金〕(hard) cash;〔口語〕dough; bread.

こ

小悪魔【こあくま】a little devil; a rogue; an imp.
◇小悪魔のような少女 a little devil [an imp] of a girl; an impish girl.

恋人【こいびと】
◇恋人いない歴⇨かのじょ
◇友達以上恋人未満 person closer than a friend, but less intimate than a lover.

公園デビュー【こうえんデビュー】*one's* park debut; the first visit to the local park or playground by a mother with her young child (to make the acquaintance of the other mothers and children).

合コン【ごうコン】〔合同コンパ〕a mixer; a gathering over food and drink at which single young people can meet people of the opposite sex. ★⇨ゲット

攻略本【こうりゃくぼん】〔ゲームソフトなどの〕a strategy guide; a book of (strategic) hints. ★特にウェブサイト上などで手順を実演しつつ教える攻略の手引きは walk-through と呼ばれる．⇨うらわざ

ゴールイン
◇彼女は長く付き合っていた男性とこの秋めでたくゴールインした．This fall she finally [safely] got married to her long-time boyfriend.

小顔【こがお】〔小さな顔〕a small face;〔化粧などで小さく見せた顔〕a little [tiny, petite] face.

◇小顔整形 face (size) [jaw] reduction surgery; cosmetic surgery to reduce the size of the face.

五月病【ごがつびょう】May (depression) syndrome; the depression [feeling of letdown] which newcomers experience in May, a month after their admission to college or employment.

コギャル a *kogyaru*; an obsessively trend-conscious teenage girl. ★⇨ギャル

こく

◇屁をこく〔卑語〕(let off a) fart.
◇うそをこくな．Liar!; I don't believe you [a word of it].
◇馬鹿こけ！ Nonsense!;〔英〕Rubbish!;〔米口語〕Bullshit!
◇ヘタこく〔どじを踏む〕(make a) blunder;〔口語〕goof up;〔俗語〕blow it. ★⇨せんずり.

告白(する)【こくはく(する)】, 告る【コクる】

◇さっさと**告白**しろよ[**コク**っちゃえよ]．まごまごしてると他の男に取られちゃうぞ．Tell her right away, or some other guy will have her.

◇彼女に愛を**告白**する勇気をくじかれた．My resolve to confess my love to her was crushed.
◇彼は思いきって彼女に**告白**した．He summoned up courage [took the plunge] and confessed his love for her.
◇衝撃の性**告白**！ これが女子高生の赤裸々な実態だ．Shocking sexual confessions! Here are the stark facts about high-school girls.

コケ
◇あいつに**コケ**にされた．He made a fool of me [treated me like a fool].

こける〔興行的に失敗する〕(be a) flop. ★⇨おおコケ
◇彼が演出した公演がこけて劇団は大赤字を背負い込んだ．His production was a flop and the company went deeply into the red.

午後一【ごごいち】
◇**午後一**で伺います．I'll come by (the) first thing in the afternoon.;〔昼休みが終わったらすぐに〕I'll come by just after lunch. ★「朝一」なら first thing in the morning となる．

五穀米【ごこくまい】mixture of five varieties of bean, grass, or cereal plant; it often includes rice, wheat, millet, or soy beans.

腰掛け【こしかけ】〔一時の身の置きどころ〕a stepping-stone (to something else).
◇この仕事は本当にやりたいことが見つかるまでの**腰掛け**にやっているまでだ．I'm only doing this job temporarily until I find something I really want to do.; This is just a temporary job till I can find a job I really want to do.
◇彼女たちにとって仕事は結婚までの**腰掛け**にすぎない．For

such girls a job is merely a temporary stage before marriage [stepping stone to marriage].
◇今の会社はほんの**腰掛け**さ．I am only working in [for] the present company temporarily [for a short time, as a temporary expedient].; I'm not staying at the present company for long.
◇この会社に就職した以上，**腰掛け**的に考えてもらっては困る．Now you've joined the company I don't expect you to treat it as a short-term expedient [I expect you to treat it as a proper, long-term job].
◇**腰掛け**仕事 a stopgap [makeshift] job; just a temporary job.

個室ビデオ【こしつビデオ】 a private-room video shop.

腰パン【こしパン】〔ズボンをずり落ちそうなほど下げてはく〕〔米俗語〕sag.

こじゃれた a bit [somewhat] stylish [chic].
◇こじゃれた感じの店 a somewhat trendy shop.

コスプレ 〔人気スター・アニメのキャラクターと同じコスチュームをして楽しむこと〕cosplay; dressing up as a favorite character from a comic, etc. ★ cosplay, cosplayer は anime, manga (⇨アニメ) などと同じように一般的な英語ではないがその世界では通用する．一般的には英語で costume play と言うと「昔の衣装をつけて演じる劇，時代劇」を意味することが多い．
◇**コスプレ**喫茶 a cosplay cafe.

コスプレイヤー cosplayer ★⇨コスプレ；person who dresses up in the apparel worn by a comic-book or manga character, a historical figure, or other creature of note.

ゴスロリ〔ゴシック・ロリータ・ファッションの略称〕"GothLoli"; "Gothic Lolita" (fashion); a fashion style combining Rococo- and Victorian-style girls' clothing with a Gothic sensibility.

午前様【ごぜんさま】 coming home after midnight [in the small hours];〔真夜中過ぎまで飲んでいる人〕a night revel(l)er (who doesn't return until the early morning).
◇このところ**午前様**続きで女房にいやな顔をされています．These days I've been coming home in the small hours night after night and my wife is fed up with me [I've been getting nasty looks from my wife].

コタツムリ warm-table slug.

こだわり
◇シェフ**こだわり**の一品 the chef's original, particular (à-la-carte) dish; the chef's pride and joy.

ゴチ[ごちそう]になる be given a meal [drink]; have a meal [drink] at ...'s (house); be invited to dinner [for a meal]; be treated to ....
◇すきやきを**ごちそう**になる have [be given, be treated to] *sukiyaki*.
◇先輩にエスニック料理を**ゴチ**になった．Older members of the club treated us to a meal of ethnic food.

◇〔飲食店などで〕それじゃあ今日はごちそうになります. Well, this time, if you insist. Thank you very much.

コテコテ
◇コテコテの大阪人 an Osakan to the core [through and through].

ご当地【ごとうち】
◇ご当地キャラ trademark plush doll, such as Little Kitty, dressed in traditional local gear or team mascot costume [suit].
◇ご当地ソング a song which names and employs the features of a particular locality; a song containing local references (aimed at gaining popularity with people from that locality).
◇ご当地ナンバー〔自動車の〕a local place-name registration number; a vehicle registration number including a newly-approved place-name.

孤独死【こどくし】dying alone [unattended]; (a) solitary death; death without anybody present.
◇大都会の真ん中で孤独死を迎える老人の数は年々増え続けている. The number of old people who die alone [entirely on their own, in complete solitude] in the middle of big cities is increasing year by year.; There is a yearly increase in the number of old people who die on their own without anybody knowing.

ゴト師【ゴトし】〔パチンコ店で不正な器具で玉を獲得する犯罪者〕a (pachinko) cheater; a person who secretly rigs gambling machines to earn a high payout.

寿退社【ことぶきたいしゃ】quitting a job in order to get married.

子供の使い【こどものつかい】
⇨ガキのつかい

コピペ〔コピー・アンド・ペースト(コピーと貼り付け)の略〕
copy and paste.

瘤付き【こぶつき】
◇こぶつきバツイチ男 a divorced guy with a kid.
◇こぶつきでクラス会に出る show up at a class reunion with a kid in tow.
◇彼の結婚相手はこぶつきだ．The one he's marrying has kids.

5本指ソックス[靴下]【ごほんゆびソックス[くつした]】
five-toe(d) socks.

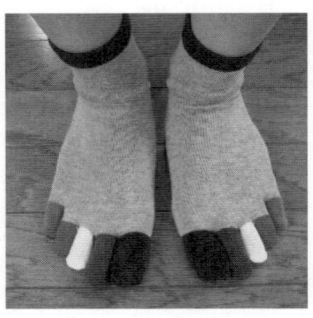

小マダム【こマダム】
wealthy and stylishly turned-out young married woman.

困ったちゃん【こまったちゃん】
a troublesome [an annoying] person; a pest; a pain in the neck [ass].
◇困ったちゃんだなあ！ What a spoiled brat!

ごみ屋敷【ごみやしき】
house, in which the owner is sometimes

living, that overflows with waste.

コミケ(ット) 〔コミックマーケットの略〕a comic market.
★漫画やアニメファンの間では a comiket でも通じる. ⇨コスプレ

コラボ(レーション)する collaborate.
✧A 社と B 社がコラボした商品 a collaborative [joint] Company A-Company B product; a product developed [designed, marketed etc.] collaboratively [jointly] by Company A and Company B
✧日産は家具メーカーとコラボレーションした自動車を販売している. Nissan is selling an automobile developed together with a furniture manufacturer.
✧ピアノと三味線のコラボレーション a duet for piano and samisen; (a) piano-samisen fusion.
✧コラボ企画 a collaborative [joint] project.
✧コラボ商品[モデル] a collaborative [joint] product [model].

壊れる【こわれる】
✧母親の虐待で彼女は少しずつ壊れていった. Little by little her mother's abuse told on her [screwed her up, fucked up her mind].
✧日ごろおとなしい彼が飲み会で完全に壊れて泣くわ, わめくわでえらい騒ぎだった. He's usually a quiet sort of person, but he totally lost it when, out carousing with friends, he started screaming and broke down in tears.

根性焼き【こんじょうやき】〔タバコの火などを肌に押し付けて強さを見せ付けること〕showing *one's* guts by stubbing *one's* cigarette out on *one's* arm.

コンパ　a social; a party.
◇新入生の歓迎コンパをやる give [throw] a party in honor of freshmen. ★⇨ごうコン，おいだしコンパ，くそ

コンパニオン　〔接待役の女性〕〔パーティーなどの〕a party hostess;〔展示会などの〕a convention guide; a trade-show hostess; booth babe [bunny].

コンパニオン立ち【コンパニオンだち】, モデル立ち【モデルだち】 booth babe pose; fashion model's pose, used also by tradeshow hostesses, in which, hand on hip, the opposite foot is pointed straight ahead and the other aslant behind it.

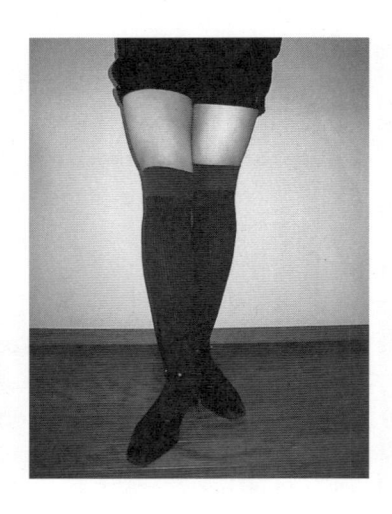

研究社の本
http://www.kenkyusha.co.jp

● 基本語重視、使いやすさにもこだわった新版
ライトハウス和英辞典 [第5版]
小島義郎・竹林 滋・中尾啓介・増田秀夫〔編〕
B6変型判 2色刷／2,730円／978-4-7674-2214-5

● 基礎の確認に、入試対策に　最新の6万7千語
ライトハウス英和辞典 [第5版]
B6変型判 2色刷 CD1枚付／3,045円／978-4-7674-1505-5

ライトハウスの上級辞典 ──
収録語句約10万。
大学入試やTOEIC®テスト受験者に最適の辞典。

明解な語法と約10万の最新語彙。
入試・実用に広く使える。

ルミナス英和辞典 [第2版]
B6変型判 2色刷／3,360円／978-4-7674-1531-4

ルミナス和英辞典 [第2版]
B6変型判 2色刷／3,570円／978-4-7674-2229-9

[CD-ROM版] ルミナス英和・和英辞典　8,820円／978-4-7674-7207-2

総収録語数10万超。累計で1200万部を超える本格派辞典！
新英和中辞典 [第7版]
・並装　3,360円／978-4-7674-1078-4
・革装　5,250円／978-4-7674-1068-5

携帯版和英辞典最大級の18万7千項目！
新和英中辞典 [第5版]
・並装　3,780円／978-4-7674-2058-5
・革装　5,565円／978-4-7674-2048-6

● 収録項目26万。最大級の語義・用例を収録した「真の大英和」！
新英和大辞典 [第6版]
竹林 滋（編集代表）
・並装 18,900円／978-4-7674-1026-5　・背革装 22,050円／978-4-7674-1016-6
・EPWING版 CD-ROM 16,800円／978-4-7674-7203-4

● 堂々の48万項目。最大・最強の和英辞典！
新和英大辞典 [第5版]
渡邉敏郎、E.Skrzypczak、P.Snowden
・並装 18,900円／978-4-7674-2026-4　・背革装 22,050円／978-4-7674-2016-5
・EPWING版 CD-ROM 16,800円／978-4-7674-7201-0

EPWING版 CD-ROM　研究社 新英和大辞典 & 新和英大辞典　26,250円／978-4-7674-7204-1

専門語から新語まで27万語をコンパクトに収録。
リーダーズ英和辞典 [第2版]
松田徳一郎〔編〕・並装 7,980円／978-4-7674-1431-7
・革装 10,500円／978-4-7674-1421-8

『リーダーズ英和辞典』を補強する19万語。
リーダーズ・プラス
松田徳一郎 ほか〔編〕
・B6変形判 10,500円／978-4-7674-1435-5

CD-ROM Windows 版　リーダーズ＋プラス GOLD　10,500円／978-4-7674-7205-8
DVD-ROM Windows 版　電子版 研究社 英語大辞典　31,500円／978-4-7674-7206-5

研究社の本
http://www.kenkyusha.co.jp

■新刊■一見やさしそうなイディオムも使い方には要注意!
日本人が使えない 英語の重要フレーズ125
ジョン・ビントリフ、森田久司〔著〕 A5判 158頁 CD付/1,680円/978-4-327-45218-6
学校では暗記しただけでは使えない基本的なイディオムの、意味の成り立ちや聞き手に与える印象、適切な使い方を伝授。ネイティブが日常的に使うフレーズも選りすぐって取り上げた。

日本人が知らない 英語の必須フレーズ150
このイディオムがわかれば、あなたもネイティブ・レベル
ジョン・ビントリフ、森田久司〔著〕 A5判 192頁/1,575円/978-4-327-45205-6

■新刊■あなたの英文法に「ダメ出し」!?
ウソのようなホントの英文法
佐久間 治〔著〕 四六判 192頁/1,470円/978-4-327-45217-9
言葉は日々刻々変化するもの。私たちが学んできた英語と食い違いを見せる英語圏の英文法の現状を、過激なまでに現実に即して軽妙に紹介する刺激的な英文法読本。

■英文法の疑問あれこれを、語源の知識を材料に解き明かす。
英文法のカラクリがわかる 佐久間 治〔著〕
A5判 200頁/1,470円/978-4-327-45190-5

■無理なく基本から積み重ねられる初級者向けの演習書
入門からの 速効音トレ 英語リスニング
安武内ひろし〔著〕 A5判 208頁 CD2枚付/2,310円/978-4-327-45216-2
母音の「ア」を「カエルのア」「あくびのア」「ゲップのア」と分けてわかりやすく説明をつけるなど初級者向けに工夫しているので、納得しながらトレーニングできる。

■シリーズ500万部突破! 英会話教本の超定番。CD付き。
アメリカ口語教本 <最新改訂版>
W. L. クラーク〔著〕 各巻CD付き

入門用	A5判 192頁/1,995円/978-4-327-44087-9 英検3級~準2級・TOEIC300~450レベル	中級用
初級用	A5判 268頁/2,415円/978-4-327-44088-6 英検準2級~2級・TOEIC 400~600レベル	上級用

■英語の思考回路が身につく、ひとクラス上の会話書。「中級編」全面改訂! 好
必ずものになる 話すための英文法 [CDブック] 市橋
● Step 5 [中級編Ⅰ] 978-4-327-45211-7 ● Step 6 [中級編Ⅱ] 978-4-327-45212-4 四六

既刊 6冊	四六判 148~156頁 各巻1470円	● 超入門編(上巻) 978-4-327-45201-7 ● 超入門編(下巻) 978-4-327-45202-5	● Step 1 [入門編Ⅰ] 978-4-327-45193 ● Step 2 [入門編Ⅱ] 978-4-327-45194

■なぜ小泉やオバマの演説は人を惹きつけるのか？
人を惹きつける「ことば戦略」
ことばのスイッチを切り替えろ！
東 照二〔著〕　四六判 236頁／1,575円／978-4-327-37725-0
テレビ番組の司会者や政治家を例に、人の心を惹きつけ、共感を呼びおこすことばの使い方とはどういうものかを、コード・スイッチングという新しい視点から考える。

■小泉首相はどこが画期的だったのか
歴代首相の言語力を診断する
東 照二〔著〕　四六判 232頁／1,470円／978-4-327-37697-0

■読むことのヒント満載！
想い出のブックカフェ　巽孝之 書評集成
巽 孝之〔著〕　四六判 386頁／2,520円／978-4-327-37724-3
何の気なしに交わされたカフェでのおしゃべりから、とてつもないアイデアがひらめくことがある。『朝日』『読売』『毎日』など新聞各紙で書評委員を務めた著者の書評集成。

■「山貞」（やまてい）の名で親しまれてきた伝説の参考書、ついに復刊！
新々英文解釈研究（新訂新版）＜復刻版＞
山崎 貞〔著〕佐山栄太郎〔改訂〕　B6判 496頁／3,150円／978-4-327-75102-9

新自修英文典（増訂新版）＜復刻版＞
山崎 貞〔著〕毛利可信〔増訂〕　B6判 608頁／3,150円／978-4-327-75101-2

頁／2,730円／978-4-327-44089-3
準1級・TOEIC 500～750Lレベル

／3,150円／978-4-327-44090-9
OEIC 700～レベル

4頁　各巻1,575円
〔初級編Ⅰ〕978-4-327-45195-9
〔初級編Ⅱ〕978-4-327-45196-7

携帯電話でリーダーズ英和辞典が引ける！
リーダーズ＋プラス英和辞典（46万語収録）に毎月約1,000語の新語を追加！

英語で困ったらすぐに携帯電話の辞書検索サイトへ。簡単な操作で手軽に辞書を引くことができます。

【NTTドコモ ｉモード】メニューリスト → 辞書・便利ツール → 辞書 → 携帯リーダーズ
【au EZweb】EZトップメニュー → カテゴリーで探す → 辞書・便利ツール → 研究社英語辞典
【SoftBank yahoo!ケータイ】メニューリスト → 辞書・ツール → 辞書 → 研究社英語辞書＋

研究社のホームページ リニューアル！

無料 辞書検索サービス開始！

http://www.kenkyusha.co.jp

ルミナス英和辞典 第2版
▶収録語句約10万。
大学入試やTOEIC®テスト受験者に最適の辞典。

ルミナス和英辞典 第2版
▶明解な語法と約10万の最新語彙。
入試・実用に広く使える。

★電子版ならではの、各種検索が可能となりました。
さらに、英語を使って活躍する方々へのインタビューなど、
新しいコンテンツの連載も始まりました。

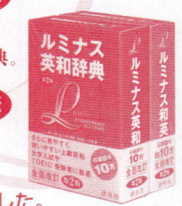

研究社のオンライン辞書検索サービス・・・・・・KOD

KOD
[ケー オー ディー]

定評ある **18**辞典を自在に検索、引き放題。毎月最新の語彙を追加。

新会員募集中！

定評のある研究社の18辞典＋「大辞林」(三省堂) が24時間いつでも利用可能。毎月、続々と追加される新項目を含め、オンラインならではの豊富な機能で自在に検索できます。
270万語の圧倒的なパワーをぜひ体感してください。
＊6ヶ月3,150円(税込み)から

http://kod.kenkyusha.co.jp

◎図書館や団体でのご加入・公費対策など、お問い合わせはお気軽にどうぞ。

●この出版案内には2009年2月現在の出版物から収録しています。
●表示の価格は定価(本体価格＋税)です。重版等により定価が変わる場合がありますのでご了承ください。
●ISBNコードはご注文の際にご利用ください。

〒102-8152 東京都千代田区富士見2-11-3 TEL 03(3288)7777 FAX 03(3288)7799 [営業]

さ

サービス残業【サービスざんぎょう】 unpaid [off-the-clock] overtime (work).
◇**サービス残業**する work overtime without pay; put in unpaid overtime.

ザーメン〔精液〕semen; sperm.

さえてる
◇今日は彼の包丁が**さえている**．He is really showing off his culinary skills today.
◇〔作品を前にして〕職人の技が**さえていますね**．This piece shows superb craftsmanship.

逆さクラゲ【さかさクラゲ】〔連れ込み旅館．温泉のマークを逆さにしたクラゲに見立てた呼び名〕a hotel catering to lovers; a hotel that rents rooms by the hour.

先振り詐欺【さきふりさぎ】 fraudulent appropriation of an advance payment for goods or services not rendered.

さくさく
◇プログラムが**サクサク**動く a computer program runs at a blazing speed [fast clip, rapid pace].

さくっと〔手早く；短時間で〕quickly; snappily; with alacrity.
◇この仕事は**さくっと**済ませちゃいましょうよ．Let's snap to it and finish the job quickly.

さくら 〔大道商人の〕a decoy; a dummy purchaser;〔俗語〕a shill; a capper;〔オークションで値段を吊り上げるための〕by-bidder.
◇さくらになる act as a decoy [by-bidder, shill].
◇さくらを使う employ a decoy [by-bidder, shill].

雑魚【ザコ】small fish; small [young] fry;〔下っぱ・小物〕small fry. ★fry は「稚魚, 小魚」の意.

サザエさん症候群【サザエさんしょうこうぐん】
〔日曜の夕方にテレビアニメ「サザエさん」が放送されるのを見て月曜に会社や学校へ行くのが嫌になること〕'Sazae syndrome' is a popular term for the melancholy many feel on the eve of a new workweek; "Sazae-san," which airs on Sunday evenings from 6:30, is a cartoon drama that celebrates traditional family values.

座敷犬【ざしきけん】〔室内犬〕an indoor dog; a house dog;〔愛玩犬〕a toy dog.

座敷童【ざしきわらし】〔東北地方に伝わる家の守り神〕the protective deity [genius loci] of a home in the Tohoku region of Japan.

差しで【さしで】〔二人きりで〕between two people;〔向かいあって〕face to face; tête-à-tête. ★ tête-à-tête は元来フランス語で「頭 (*tête*) と頭を向け合って (話すこと)」の意.
◇差しで飲む have a drink just for two;〔向かいあって〕sit across from each other and drink .
◇(…と)差しで話し合う〔二人だけで〕one-on-one conversation; have a tête-à-tête (with . . .).

授かり婚【さずかりこん】〔花嫁がすでに妊娠している状態での結婚〕a wedding [marriage] with the bride (already) pregnant [with a baby on the way]; a wedding [marriage] where the bride is (already) pregnant; an enforced [a hurried] wedding [marriage] (because a baby is on the way). ★⇨できちゃったけっこん, おめでたこん

サツ〔警察〕the police;〔口語で集合的に「おまわり, デカ」〕the cops;〔俗語〕the fuzz; the pigs.
◇サツだ！ Here come the cops!
◇サツ回りの記者 a news reporter on the police beat.

サビ抜き【サビぬき】(sushi) without wasabi.

サビ残【サビざん】⇨サービスざんぎょう

さぶいぼ, 寒疣 〔鳥肌〕 gooseflesh; goose bumps; goose pimples.
✧さぶいぼができる〔ぞっとする〕get goose bumps [pimples];〔興奮・感動でぞくぞくする〕be thrilled [electrified]; feel a thrill.

サプライズ
✧彼女が選んだ閣僚の顔ぶれには**サプライズ**が全く[ほとんど]なかった．There were no [a few] surprises in her choice of cabinet members.

寒い【さむい】〔貧弱な〕poor; miserable; pathetic.
✧**寒い**ギャグ a bad [weak, feeble] joke.
✧**寒い**冗談を言う make a weak [feeble] joke.
✧「足を踏んでも悪しからず」「さむー！」"I hope you'll forgive me for giving you sore toes." "Cor-ny!" ★前半は forgive と for giving をかけたしゃれ．corny は俗語で「古臭い」の意．

サムターン回し【サムターンまわし】〔泥棒の鍵こじあけの手口〕opening [forcing open] a thumbturn (from the other side of the door).

サラ金【サラきん】〔サラリーマン向けの金融〕financing [loans] for white-collar [salaried] workers; consumer financing [loans];〔金融会社〕a consumer financing firm; a personal finance company;〔高利貸し〕a loan shark (who preys on white-collar workers). ★⇨やみ
✧**サラ金**地獄 loan-shark hell; the plight of people in debt to loan sharks.

ざる, 笊
◇私，見掛けによらず，**ザル**なんです．I may not look (like) it, but I can drink a lot.

三角食べ 【さんかくたべ】
〔食事の時，主食→おかず→汁物のように順番に食べること〕"triangle eating"; taking something alternately from each dish on the table.

3K 【さんケー】
〔きつい・きたない・危険(な仕事)〕the 3 Ds: demanding [difficult], dirty, and dangerous jobs.

三ケツ 【さんケツ】
〔自転車・バイクなどの三人乗り〕three asses on one「bicycle [motorscooter]．★⇨にケツ

残念会 【ざんねんかい】，残念パーティ 【ざんねんパーティ】
consolation party; better-luck-next-time party; booby-prize party.

3秒ルール 【さんびょうルール】
〔落とした食べ物は3秒以内に拾えば食べられるという俗信〕three second rule. ★英語ではしばしば5秒ルール (five second rule) となる．

し

幸せ太り【しあわせぶとり】putting on weight [getting fat] with contentment.

シカトする ignore; ostracize; leave ... out; exclude ... from among a group; cut ... dead [cold].

自家発電【じかはつでん】⇨せんずり

自虐ネタ【じぎゃくネタ】masochistic jokes that rely for their bite on a fund of unhappy personal experiences.

しごく ⇨せんずり

自己中, 自己チュー【じこチュー】
✧最近**自己中**な大人が目立って多い. Lately a conspicuously large number of grown-ups are self-centered.
✧**自己チュー**なやつだ. He believes in looking out for number one [No. 1].

仕込み【しこみ】⇨やらせ

事故る【じこる】have [cause] a traffic [car] accident.

事実婚【じじつこん】a de facto marriage; marriage without registration.

時事ネタ【じじネタ】material for essays or humorous pieces

drawn from current issues or events.

実弾 【じつだん】 〔買収用などの現金〕 money; cash.
◇実弾の偉力 the influence of money.
◇選挙に実弾を使う try to buy (off) votes in an election.

室内犬 【しつないけん】 ⇨ざしきけん

シネコン，シネマ・コンプレックス 〔複合型映画館〕
a cinema complex.

シノギ 〔暴力団が資金を得る手段〕 a source of income [a moneymaker] for a gang.

しばく ⇨どつく

自爆テロ 【じばくテロ】
◇自爆テロを実行する carry out a (terrorist) suicide bombing.
◇自爆テロに巻き込まれる get involved in a suicide bombing.
◇自爆テロ犯 a suicide bomber.

自分探し 【じぶんさがし】 the search for self [self-realization, an identity].
◇彼は自分探しの旅に出た．He set off on a journey to find out who he really is [a journey in pursuit of his self].
◇自分探しをする try and discover *one's* (true) identity.

地味婚 【じみこん】 a simple [a modest, an unflashy, an unpretentious] wedding.
◇地味婚ですますつもりだ．Our wedding will be a simple affair.

シメシメ, しめた
Got it!; It's in the bag!; Bingo!; 〔発見して〕Eureka!

◇しめた. 抜け道があったぞ！ Got it! [Yahoo!] I found a secret passage [path].; Eureka! Secret exit [way out]!

◇これがうまく行きゃしめたものだ. If I succeed in this, I'm made.

シメる, 締[絞]める

◇生意気な新入生を**シメる** come down hard on a cocky new student; haze a cocky new student.

◇飲んだ後ラーメンで**締める** top off a night on the town with a bowl of hot Chinese noodles.

しも, 下
〔下半身〕the lower part of the body; the abdomen; 〔陰部〕*one's* private parts; the privates; the genitals; 〔排泄〕*one's* bowel functions; excretion. ★⇨かはんしん

◇下の世話をする help ... with his bowel functions; clean ... up after he has been to the toilet; change ...'s diapers; tend [attend] to ...'s bodily [personal] needs.

◇下の話で恐縮ですが if you will forgive me for mentioning a personal subject [bringing up a matter like this].

◇下ネタ an indecent [an improper, a bawdy, a dirty, a lewd, an obscene] topic [subject].

ジモティー
a local; a townie.

シャカシャカ音【シャカシャカおん】

◇彼のイヤホンから**シャカシャカ音**が漏れるのが神経にさわった. The irritating sound from his earphones got on my nerves.

ジャケ買い【ジャケがい】〔ジャケットが気に入っただけで CD などを買ってしまうこと〕buying [purchasing] (a CD) only because of the jacket [cover, sleeve].

シャコタン，車高短 〔暴走族の車などで車高を低く改造したもの〕a lowered car; a lowrider.

じゃ（じゃ）ーん 〔自慢げに物を見せるときの間投詞〕Ta-da!
★発音は「タダー」に近い．

シャッター通り[商店街]【シャッターどおり[しょうてんがい]】a shuttered shopping mall; a street with many closed stores [shops].

シャネラー a (young) woman who wears [uses] only Chanel-brand goods; a Chanel fanatic.

シャバ，娑婆 〔刑務所・軍隊などからみた外の世界〕the outside world.
◇(受刑者が)シャバに出る[戻る] get out of prison; get back into the outside world; be back on the street.
◇もうシャバには用がない．I have no more use for this world.; There is nothing more for me to do in this life.
◇もう一度シャバの空気を吸いたい．I want to breathe in once more the air in the outside world.

ジャパニメーション 〔日本製アニメ〕Japanimation; anime; animation films made in Japan [of Japanese make].
★⇨アニメ

シャブ〔覚醒剤〕〔俗語〕speed; an upper; a pep pill.

喋り倒す【しゃべりたおす】〔しゃべりまくる〕jabber away; babble on;〔相手を圧倒する勢いでしゃべる〕talk ...'s ear off ★「相手の耳が取れるまでしゃべる」の意; rattle on.
◇たまの休日は女友達とただもうしゃべり倒すのが私の息抜き. On my rare days off I let off steam by just jabbering away with my girl friends.
◇彼はシンポジウムに呼ばれて，2時間しゃべり倒した. He was invited to the symposium and rattled on unstoppably for two solid hours. ★⇨…たおす

写メ(ール)【しゃメ(ール)】〔写真メール〕(a) photo e-mail;〔商標名〕Sha-Mail.

就活【しゅうかつ】, 就職活動【しゅうしょくかつどう】
job hunting (activities); steps followed by college students in seeking employment.
◇就職活動で忙しい be busy seeking employment; be busy job hunting.
◇就職活動をする do job-hunting; hunt for work.

充電【じゅうでん】

◇携帯電話(用)緊急**充電**器 a boost(ing) charger for a cellphone. ★⇨ケータイ

◇この携帯はフル**充電**でも3日しかもたない．This cellphone lasts only three days (even) on a full charge [when fully charged].

◇**充電**スタンド〔携帯電話などの〕a charging [charge] cradle (for a cellular phone).

◇いい仕事をするためには，ときどき休みを取って**充電**する必要がある．If you want to do good work, every once in a while you've got to take some time off to recharge (your batteries).

◇彼はいま執筆を休んで**充電**期間中だ．He's taking a break from writing and recharging his batteries.

◇彼女は一年間の**充電**期間を取ってから活動を再開した．After taking a year off to recharge, she resumed her active work schedule.

十八禁【じゅうはちきん】

〔掲示で,「十八歳未満入場禁止」〕Admittance denied to those under 18.;〔未成年者入場禁止〕No Admission to Minors; No Minors Admitted;〔成人向け〕(for) adults only. ★⇨アダルト

COLUMN

米国では「17禁」,「お酒は21になってから」?

米国の映画の年齢制限は以下のように分類されている．

G　　　一般向け (general).
PG　　親の指導 (parental guidance) が望ましい．
PG-13　13歳未満は親の指導が望ましい．
R　　　年齢制限あり (restricted). 17歳未満は保護者の付き添いが必要．
NC-17　17歳およびそれ未満入場禁止．元来は「17禁未満禁止 (no children under 17)」の略だったが，現在は「18禁」と同じになっている．また，かつてはXという表示だったので今でも成人向け映画をX-rated filmと呼ぶことがある．

> このほかテレビ番組やゲームソフトにも似たような分類がついていることが多い．
> ちなみに法的に成人扱いされる年齢は州や分野によって違うが 18 歳以上の所が多い．しかし飲酒が許されるのは全国一律に 21 歳以上と決まっている．ただし保護者同伴などの条件付きでそれ未満でも許される州もある．

週末起業(家)【しゅうまつきぎょう(か)】 a business operated by a salaried worker on weekends; weekend business (person).

週末婚【しゅうまつこん】〔夫婦が週末だけ一緒に生活をする結婚形態〕a weekend marriage; weekend wedlock.

熟女【じゅくじょ】a mature woman.

熟年離婚【じゅくねんりこん】(a) late divorce.

ジュワ(ー)ッと
◇(口に)ジュワッと広がる味 a flavorsome rush (spreads through one's mouth).

瞬間芸【しゅんかんげい】⇨いっぱつげい

正月太り【しょうがつぶとり】New Year's waist.
◇正月太りする put on weight at New Year's. ★⇨ふゆぶとり

上等【じょうとう】
◇上等じゃねえか．〔挑発を受けて〕It's OK [fine] by me!; Gee, you really scare me!
◇喧嘩上等 I never run from [turn my back on] a fight.

勝負服【しょうぶふく】〔ここ一番というときに着る服〕*one's* lucky clothes [outfit, suit].

女王様【じょおうさま】〔SMの〕dominatrix; mistress.

食育【しょくいく】〔栄養教育〕nutrition education;〔正しい食生活を通じて健全な心身を育むこと〕diet [dietary] education.
◇**食育**基本法 the Basic Law for Food Education.

食玩【しょくがん】〔菓子などのおまけになる小型玩具〕a candy toy.

女子【じょし】
◇教室の掃除くらい**女子**[男子]にやらせとけばいいじゃん．We should just make the girls [boys] clean up the classroom.
◇**女子**[女性]アナ（ウンサー） a woman [female, lady] announcer.

ショタコン〔少年に性的関心を抱くこと〕a sexual interest in [a sexual preference for] young boys; boy love;〔小児性愛者〕pedophile. ★⇨ロリコン

ショバ代，所場代【しょばだい】the money charged for space [a booth, a stall] at a fair [flea market, market, bazaar].

しょぼい〔みすぼらしい〕shabby; dull;〔気の滅入る〕gloomy; miserable-looking[-sounding]; depressing.
◇彼はしょぼい車に乗っていた．He was driving a sorry-looking car.
◇彼のいうことはいつもしょぼい．The things he says are so depressing.

地雷【じらい】
✧**地雷を踏む** step on a (land) mine;〔比喩的に〕meet with an unexpected disaster.

シロガネーゼ
〔東京・白金周辺に住む金持ちの主婦〕a wealthy woman who lives in Shirogane, Tokyo; a "Shiroganese."

人前結婚式【じんぜんけっこんしき】
〔特定宗教によらない結婚式〕secular [non-religious] wedding.

心霊【しんれい】
✧**心霊現象** a spiritualist(ic) [psychic(al)] phenomenon.
✧**心霊写真** a spirit photograph; a psychograph.
✧**心霊療法** psychic healing.
✧**心霊スポット** a psychic [haunted] spot.

す

数字【すうじ】
◇**数字**が取れる(=視聴率のよい)番組[タレント] program [celebrity] with excellent drawing power [with high audience ratings].
◇**数字**を持ってる脚本家[ディレクター] scriptwriter who can put up the numbers; director with a good track record.
◇**数字**の取れないギャラ泥棒 actor or celebrity who demands a higher guarantee than his numbers warrant.

スープ
◇娘夫婦は**スープ**の冷めない距離に住んでいる．My daughter and her husband live just around the corner.

すかしっ屁【すかしっぺ】a silent fart.
◇**すかしっ屁**をひる break wind [fart] noiselessly. ★⇨こく

すかす〔気取る，すます〕be affected; put on airs; pose.

隙間産業【すきまさんぎょう】a niche industry; a niche business.

スキミング〔クレジットカードの磁気情報を盗む犯罪〕(credit card) skimming.

スクール水着【スクールみずぎ】 a school swimsuit.

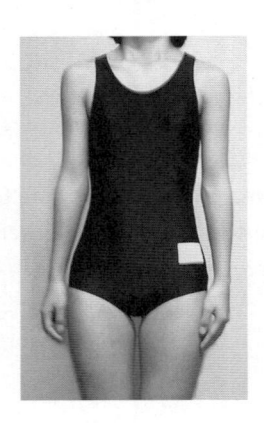

スグレもの〔すぐれた物〕an outstanding [a superior, a great] thing;〔利用価値の高い品物〕a highly useful product.

スケ番【スケばん】〔女番長〕a cuddle-bunny leader.

スケベ，助平 〔好色な男〕a lecherous [lewd] person; a lecher; a satyr.
◇スケベな bawdy; lecherous; lewd; lustful; lascivious;〔俗語〕horny.
◇助平じじい a dirty old man; an old goat.
◇ど助平 a real lecher; a sex fiend; a pervert;〔口語〕a perv.
◇ど助平な filthy; perverted.
◇助平根性〔好色〕lechery; lewdness;〔貪欲〕greed.
◇助平根性を起こす[出す] be prompted by [act from] selfish motives
◇助平根性を起こして相場に手を出して大損した．Prompted by greed, he had a flutter on the stock market and lost a lot of money.

ずたぼろに into pieces [shreds].
◇敵にずたぼろにされる be wiped out by an opponent.
◇離婚でズタボロになる be torn up over a divorce.
◇私は彼とかかわったために身も心もずたぼろにされてしまった．My involvement with him left me wiped out [in tatters] both physically and mentally.

スッチー 〔スチュワーデス〕a [an airplane] stewardess; a flight attendant.

スッピン
◇スッピンだ wear no makeup; have no makeup on.

ストーカー 〔しつこくつけ回す人〕a stalker.
◇娘がストーカーの被害にあっている．My daughter is being stalked.
◇ストーカー行為 stalking.
◇ストーカー殺人 (a) stalking [stalker] murder.

ストライク(ゾーン)

◇あいつは女性の**ストライクゾーン**が狭い[広い]. His tastes in women are narrow [broad].

◇この小説はあまり期待せずに買ったのだが，読んでみたらど**ストライク**で(＝好みにぴったりで)一気読みしてしまった．I bought a copy of the novel on a whim. But I was immediately hooked and read it cover to cover at a single sitting.

ストラップ ⇨ケータイ

ズベ公【ずべこう】 a delinquent girl; a girl gone astray.

滑り込みセーフ【すべりこみセーフ】

◇「今朝は学校に遅刻しなかった？」「2分前で**滑り込みセーフ**だった」"Weren't you late to school this morning?" "Just made it, with two minutes to spare."

滑る【すべる】〔入試に〕fail (in) an examination;〔口語〕flunk an examination;〔口語〕be ploughed [get plucked] in an examination.

◇大学に**滑る** fail to [do not] get into a university; be rejected [turned down] by a university.

◇**滑り止め**にQ大学も受験する take the entrance examination to Q. University as a safety measure.

◇ギャグが完全に**すべった**．The joke went over like a lead balloon.; Her joke was a dud; His attempt at a jokey remark was met with silence.

スポ根【スポこん】〔スポーツ根性〕fighting spirit (in sports).
◇スポ根物 a sports-hero story.

ズラ ⇨ヅラ

ずらかる ⇨トンズラ

スリミング・コスメ〔塗った部分が痩せると称する塗布剤〕(a) slimming treatment [lotion, gel].

スルーする〔英語の through から「無視する，飛ばす」の意〕skip; ignore; pass by.

ズルズルベッタリ
◇ずるずるべったりの関係 a relationship that drags on and on and is hard to break up.
◇はじめ１晩泊めてやると言っただけなのに，ずるずるべったりと居ついてしまった．At first I said she could stay for just a night, but she has stayed on with us ever since.
◇ずるずるべったりにそこの奥さんになってしまった．She stuck with him till she became his wife.

スロー・フード〔ファースト・フードに対し〕slow food.
◇スローフード運動 the slow food movement.

せ

税金泥棒【ぜいきんどろぼう】a person living off other people's taxes; a tax parasite.

正常位【せいじょうい】the normal position [posture]; 〔口語〕the missionary position. ★「宣教師（missionary）が勧めるようなお行儀のいい体位」の意.

性同一性障害【せいどういつせいしょうがい】a gender identity disorder（略称 GID）.

セクハラ〔性的いやがらせ〕sexual harassment. ★⇨パワハラ
◇職場での**セクハラ** sexual harassment in [at] the office [workplace].
◇**セクハラ**の被害者 a victim of sexual harassment
◇**セクハラ**の加害者 a sexual harasser.
◇**セクハラ**を受ける be sexually harassed.
◇逆**セクハラ** reverse sexual harassment.
◇**セクハラ**疑惑 an allegation [a suspicion] of sexual harassment.
◇**セクハラ**で…を訴える sue . . . for sexual harassment.
◇**セクハラ**で訴えられる be sued for [accused of] sexual harassment.
◇彼［彼女］は**セクハラ**で有罪となった．He [She] was found guilty of sexual harassment.
◇そのような行為は**セクハラ**とみなされうる．Such behavior can be regarded [viewed] as sexual harassment.
◇**セクハラ**・ガイドライン sexual harassment guidelines.
◇**セクハラ**裁判 a sexual harassment trial.

◇セクハラ訴訟 a sexual harassment (law) suit.
◇セクハラ保険 sexual harassment insurance.
◇環境型セクハラ hostile environment sexual harassment.
◇対価型セクハラ quid pro quo sexual harassment.

セコい〔けちくさい〕tight-fisted; stingy;〔口語〕chintzy; cheap;〔みみっちい・いじましい〕small-minded; petty.

◇セコい考え petty thinking.
◇セコい根性 a small-minded nature; a mean spirit.
◇セコいやつ a miser;〔口語〕a skinflint; a cheapskate;〔米〕a tightwad; a penny pincher.

セコハン

◇セコハンもの used goods.
◇…をセコハンで買う buy ... secondhand [at second hand].
◇セコハンのカメラ a secondhand camera.

セックスフレンド, セフレ   a bed mate; a friend for sex; a sex(ual) partner.

セルライト   cellulite.

セレブ   a celeb(rity); a big name; a notable; a wel-known [famous] person; a public figure.

◇セレブ御用達のレストラン a restaurant that caters to celebrities;〔セレブの隠れ家的な〕a celebrity hideout.
◇あいつはセレブ気取りだ．He behaves as though he is a celebrity.
◇セレブる〔有名人の生活を味わう〕experience the life of a celebrity.

全開【ぜんかい】 ⇨パワーぜんかい

全共闘世代【ぜんきょうとうせだい】 the generation of the Joint Struggle Committee, alternatively known as *dankai no sedai* (the generation of the statistical leap [in births]), who were among the membership comprising the Joint Struggle Committee, or *Zenkyoto*, which was a student political organization opposed to the US-Japan Treaty of Mutual Cooperation and Security and which was active for a decade or so roughly straddling the period of the mid 1960s to mid 1970s.

全クリ【ぜんクリ】, 全面クリア【ぜんめんクリア】
◇全クリする〔ゲームで〕clear all the stages (of a video game); 〔クイズで〕answer correctly all the questions on a test. ★⇨クリアする

先公【せんこう】 a damn teacher;〔口語〕a teach.

センズリ, 千擦り
◇センズリをこく masturbate;〔俗語〕jerk off; toss off. ★⇨オナペット

洗濯板【せんたくいた】
◇洗濯板のような胸 a chest with the ribs showing through; a washboard chest. ★⇨ひんにゅう

全面クリア【ぜんめんクリア】 ⇨ぜんクリ

戦力外通告【せんりょくがいつうこく】〔プロスポーツなどの契約交渉時の〕(a) notification of noninclusion (in a team) [intent not to make a contract (with a player)].

❖**戦力外通告**を受ける receive notification of noninclusion.
❖彼は**戦力外通告**を受けた．He was told that he had not been chosen to play.

そ

総スカン【そうスカン】
◇彼は先生に告げ口してクラスの皆に**総スカン**を食った. The whole class froze him out [sent him to Coventry] for snitching to the teacher.

ソープ(ランド)
a massage parlor; a bathhouse (where customers pay for sex); a "soapland";〔売春宿〕a brothel; a whorehouse.
◇ソープ嬢 a bathhouse ["soapland"] hostess; a (female) sex worker.

ゾク，族
⇨ぼうそうぞく，レディース

粗大ゴミ【そだいゴミ】
(an item of) bulky [large-size(d), oversized] rubbish [trash];〔家事で役に立たない男〕a useless man about the house.
◇定年を過ぎた夫が妻から**粗大ごみ**扱いされるケースもある. There are cases where husbands after retirement are treated as (so much) oversized trash by their wives.

そっくりさん
a look-alike; a double.
◇エルヴィス・プレスリーの**そっくりさん** an Elvis Presley look-alike.
◇マリリン・モンロー**そっくりさん**コンテスト a Marilyn Monroe look-alike contest.

そっくり食品【そっくりしょくひん】
mock food.

ソッコーで，速攻で immediately; at once; right away; straightaway.
◇今夜は見たいテレビがあるからソッコーで帰るよ．There's a program I want to watch on TV tonight, so I'm going to go straight home.
◇速攻で痩せる究極のダイエット！ The ultimate diet that lets you slim down quickly [in a flash, without waiting]!

ソフビ人形【ソフビにんぎょう】〔ソフトビニール製の〕PVC figure [doll]．★PVCは塩化ビニール（polyvinyl chloride）の略．
⇨フィギュア

そもそも論【そもそもろん】
◇今更そもそも論を言う（＝問題が起きた原因や責任の所在を追及する）より具体的な対策を考えるべきだ．Now is the time to work out a practical response to the problem, not to attach blame for its cause.

剃り（込み）【ソリ（こみ）】 wearing one's hair shaved in a V at either side of the forehead; formerly common among hoods and hoodlums.

それを言っちゃあおしまいよ ⇨おしまい

ゾロ品【ゾロひん】〔新薬と同じ有効成分を含む後発［ジェネリック］医薬品〕a generic drug; a generic prescription drug; a branded generic drug;〔集合的に〕generics.

そんじょそこら

◇そんじょそこらにある代物とは違う．This is no ordinary run-of-the-mill article.; This is not the kind of article you can find just anywhere.

◇あんな才能のあるやつはそんじょそこらにはいない．You can't find talented guys like him any old where.

◇そんじょそこらの安アパートと思われちゃ困る．I don't want it to be thought of as any old (run-of-the-mill) cheap apartment block.

た

体育【たいいく】
◇体育会 an athletic(s) [a sports] association [club].
◇体育会系の学生 a sports-oriented student;〔英〕a sporty type;〔口語〕a jock.
◇体育会系のノリにはついていけない．The enthusiasm of the sports-minded types is more than I can handle.
◇体育座りする sit on the ground with *one's* arms around *one's* knees.

ダイエット
◇ダイエット(を)する[している] go [be] on a diet.
◇リンゴダイエット〔リンゴだけ食べ続ける〕an apple diet; an apple-only diet.
◇今ダイエット中なの．I'm on a diet at the moment.
◇ダイエットに成功[失敗]する succeed [fail] with a diet; succeed in sticking [fail to stick] to a diet; succeed in losing [fail to lose] weight.
◇ダイエット食品 a diet food; a slimming food [product].
◇弁当箱ダイエット〔米・おかず・野菜を3・1・2の割合で詰めた弁当で昼食を取る〕a lunch-box diet (based on packing a lunch box with three parts rice, one part main dish and two parts vegetables).
◇低インシュリンダイエット〔食事療法によって体内のインシュリンの分泌量を低く抑えることにより，結果的に体脂肪を減らすことを図るダイエット法〕a low insulin diet (略称 LID).

大根足[脚]【だいこんあし】plump [thick, stout] legs.

大根役者【だいこんやくしゃ】 a bad [poor, ham] actor; a ham.
◇あれでは**大根役者**の演技と言われても仕方ない．Hammy is the only way to describe the actor's performance.

大好き人間【だいすきにんげん】
◇チョコアイス**大好き人間** a chocolate ice cream man. ★⇨フェチ

大統領【だいとうりょう】
◇いよっ！**大統領**！〔米〕Way to go, man!; 〔英〕Brilliant [Great, Wow]!; That's the way!

タイマン 〔1対1のけんか〕a one-on-one fight [argument]; a grudge match.

…倒す【…たおす】〔徹底的にする〕do to the fullest; do completely; do thoroughly; 〔口語〕do to the max.
◇遊び**倒す** enjoy *oneself* to the fullest.
◇私は夫と南の島で2週間を遊び**倒す**のが夢でした．I always wanted to go to an island in the south with my husband and have our fill of fun for two weeks.
◇聞き**倒す** listen completely; listen to all of ....
◇英語の朗読CDを聞き**倒した**おかげでリスニングに強くなった．Because I listened to everything on some English spoken-word CDs, my listening skills improved.
◇寝**倒す** sleep until the cows come home; sleep for a long time.
◇ぼけ**倒す** keep acting like an idiot [a fool].
◇誉め**倒す** praise ... to the skies. ★⇨しゃべりたおす，つかいたおす

タカビーな 〔高飛車な，お高くとまった〕proud; haughty;

arrogant; overbearing;〔口語〕stuck up; uppish; uppity.

抱き枕【だきまくら】a body pillow; a comforter.

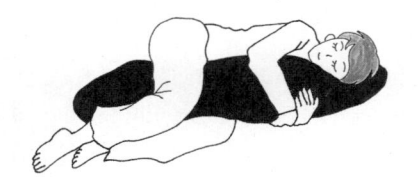

宅飲み【たくのみ】drinking at home with friends (in stead of going to a bar).

タコ足配線【たこあしはいせん】octopus wiring; plugging many leads into one (electrical) outlet; a spaghetti junction (of leads from one outlet).
◇タコ足配線にする have many electrical cords connected to a single outlet.

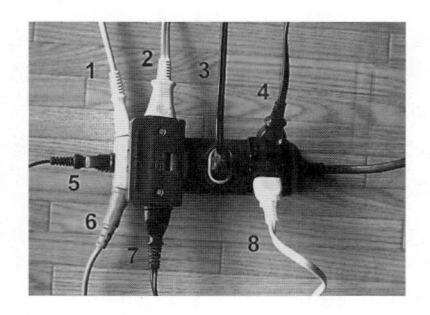

ダサい，ダサダサ tacky; tasteless; unrefined; provincial; boring; dull; square; corny; not cool; naff.

◇ダサい服装 dowdy clothes; a tasteless, unfashionable way of dressing.
◇ダサい言葉 an out-of-date [a country-like] expression.
◇ダサいやつ a geek; a nerd; a dull person.
◇今時ブランド品で着飾るなんてダサい．Wearing designer brands is out [not cool] right now.
◇「ナウい」を連発するのはもうダサいよ．The fashion for calling everything "fab" has long gone.; Calling everything "fab" is really out of date now. ★ fab は「すばらしい」の意の，ひと昔前の流行語．
◇なにあの服！ ダサダサ！ Will you look at those clothes! How ticky-tacky!

ダチ(公) 【ダチ(こう)】
◇…のダチ one of . . .'s friends [pals, crew]. ★⇨マブダチ

立ちこぎする 【たちこぎする】
〔自転車を〕pedal a bicycle standing; get up out of the saddle;〔ぶらんこを〕swing standing up.

立ちション 【たちション】，立ち小便 【たちしょうべん】
◇立ちションする urinate outdoors [by the roadside, against a wall, against a tree].
◇〔看板で〕立ち小便禁止．No Urinating.; Refrain from urinating here.

タッパ，立端
〔高さ〕height.
◇タッパがある be tall.

脱力 【だつりょく】
◇脱力キャラ an easy-going [a good-natured] person; a person

with a laidback attitude (to life). ★⇨ゆるキャラ
◇**脱力**(系)ギャグ a joke so silly [absurd] that it makes you laugh in spite of yourself.

タテノリ，縦乗り
〔リズムに合わせて体を上下に動かしたり飛び跳ねたりすること〕the pogo; jumping up and down to the beat of the music.

ダフ屋【ダフや】
a (ticket) scalper.

ダブる
〔留年する〕repeat a course [year]; do a course [year] again [all over].

ダブルハッピー婚【ダブルハッピーこん】⇨おめでたこん

ダブル不倫【ダブルふりん】
an (extra-marital) affair between a married man and a married woman. ★⇨うわき

ダベる
gab; gas; chew the fat [rag];〔英〕natter;〔米俗語〕shoot the breeze.

玉の輿【たまのこし】
◇玉の輿に乗る marry into wealth; get married to a man of wealth [high status].
◇玉の輿に乗ろうと必死になる try as hard as she can to marry into wealth.
◇玉の輿を逃す miss an opportunity to marry into wealth. ★⇨ぎゃくたま

タメ
〔同年齢〕
◇あいつとは**タメ**(年)だ．I'm the same age as he is.

◇…にタメ口をきく speak in *one's* peer language (to . . . who is not a peer).

駄目【だめ，ダメ】

◇自分の**ダメ**さ加減がわかってきた．I've come to realize how worthless [how hopeless, what a loser] I am.

◇**だめ**なやつ，**ダメ**人間 a useless [hopeless] fellow; a good-for-nothing

◇**ダメ**男[女] a worthless [lousy] man [woman];〔俗語〕a loser.
★⇨ダメンズ

駄目出し【だめだし】

◇**だめ**出しをする〔演技をやり直させる〕call for a rerun [another run-through, a retake];〔文句をつける〕point out faults [mistakes].

◇その演出家は，言葉で**だめ**出しをする前に舞台に灰皿を投げつける．Before calling for another run-through the director throws an ashtray onto the stage.

駄目元【ダメもと】

◇**ダメもと**でやってみる attempt on the assumption that it won't do any harm [it'll be all the same].

◇**ダメもと**で応募する put in an application with the attitude that it won't do any harm (to apply).

◇その作家に書いてくれるか**ダメもと**で交渉してみることにした．I decided to negotiate with that author with the attitude that it wouldn't do any harm to ask her to write something for us.

ダメンズ 〔ダメ男たち〕worthless [lousy] men;〔俗語〕male losers.

たられば〔仮定〕the "if onlies"; the "(would haves, could haves, and) should haves."
◇今さらたらればの話をしてもしょうがない. "If only" stories won't do you any good now.; It's too late to talk about "should haves."

垂れ込み【たれこみ】a tip-off; (secret) information (to the police).
◇(…を密告する)たれ込みの手紙 a letter giving information (against ...).
◇匿名のたれ込み電話があった. There was an anonymous telephone tip-off.; Police were tipped off by an anonymous phone call.

だろう運転【だろううんてん】〔「前の車は急ブレーキをかけたりしないだろう」などの勝手な思い込みで危ない運転をすること〕"it-won't-happen-to-me" driving; (dangerous) driving based on unjustified optimism [the premise, "it won't happen to me"].

団塊【だんかい】
◇団塊の世代 the baby boomers; the baby boom generation [cohort].
◇団塊ジュニア a baby-boom junior; a child of baby-boomers.

男子【だんし】⇨じょし

断トツ【だんトツ】〔断然トップ〕far and away the most [best]; a decisive [runaway, clear] lead. ★⇨ぶっちぎり
◇断トツ(1位)で折り返す make the turn (in first place) far ahead of the pack.
◇断トツ(の)1位 in first place by a decisive [runaway, clear] lead

◇断トツの人気 a runaway popularity
◇断トツで優勝する run away with the championship.

ダンパ〔ダンスパーティー〕a dance (party); a ball;〔米国の大学・高校の卒業・進学を祝う〕a prom.
◇ダンパに行く go to a dance.

タンマ〔「タイム！」の崩れた幼児語〕"King's X [Ex, Excuse, Cross]!; "Truce!"
◇タンマをかける call "Truce!"

ち

小さな親切【ちいさなしんせつ】a small kindness; a little act of kindness.
◇彼女にとって彼の**小さな親切**は大きなお世話だった．The little favors he did were a big annoyance to her.

チーマー "teamers"; juvenile delinquents frequenting the streets of Tokyo.

チーママ〔バーのマダム2人のうちの若いほう〕the junior mistress (of a bar).

チェックする keep a close watch (on . . .); follow . . . 's every move.
◇あの俳優の出演するドラマは全部**チェックしている**．She never misses a single drama that that actor appears in.
◇その歌手の服装を細かく**チェックして**取り入れる．She notes every detail of that singer's costume and incorporates it into her own wardrobe.
◇あの子，今度来た数学の先生もう**チェックしてる**よ．She's already got her beady eye on the new math teacher!

チェリーボーイ〔童貞の男〕male virgin ★英語の virgin は男女共に指す．cherry は「処女」「童貞」の象徴で，lose *one's* cherry「処女[童貞]を失う，初体験する」のような成句もある．

チキンレース (a game of) chicken.
◇対向車と**チキンレース**をする play chicken with an oncoming

チクる　tell [tattle] on ....
◇おれのことを**チク**ったのはあいつだ．He is the one who told on me.

チケットゲッター〔組織的に人気チケットを買い占める業者〕professional on-line ticket broker [scalper].

チチンプイプイ〔手品などで〕(Hey) presto!; hocus-pocus.

地デジ【ちデジ】〔地上デジタル放送〕digital terrestrial [terrestrial digital] broadcasting.
◇**地デジ**チューナー a digital terrestrial [terrestrial digital] tuner.

チャイドル〔アイドルである子供〕a child star [entertainer].

チャカ〔ピストル〕a pistol;〔口語〕a gat.

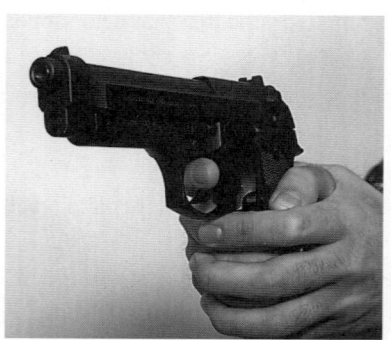

チャキチャキの〔生粋の〕trueborn; out and out; thoroughbred; pure; genuine.
◇**チャキチャキ**の江戸っ子 a trueborn "Edokko."

着うた【ちゃくうた】〔歌が流れる着メロ〕a ring song.

着声【ちゃくごえ】〔携帯電話の着信音に声を使ったもの〕a voice ringtone.

着信【ちゃくしん】〔電話の〕an incoming call.
◇**着信**音〔電話の〕a ringtone [ringer tone].
◇**着信**メロディー⇨ちゃくメロ，ちゃくうた
◇**着信**履歴[記録]〔携帯電話などの〕a record [log] of incoming calls [calls received].
◇**着信**拒否⇨ちゃっきょ
◇**着信**ボイス⇨ちゃくごえ．

着メロ【ちゃくメロ】〔電話の〕a phone melody; a ringtone melody.
◇**着メロ**サイト a ringtone (Web) site.

着拒【ちゃっきょ】〔特定の相手からの着信を拒否する機能〕call blocking [screening].

チャット (online) chat
◇**チャット**占い fortune-telling on a chat site.

茶髪【ちゃぱつ】brown-dyed hair.

チャラ
◇借金を**チャラ**にする cancel [forget] ...'s debt.
◇この話は**チャラ**にしよう．Let's forget what we said.

チャリ(ンコ)〔自転車〕bike; bicycle.
◇**チャリ**通学[通勤] bicycling to school [work]; commuting by

チャンチャン

bicycle. ★⇨ママチャリ, げんチャリ

チャンチャン
◇新品のテレビが映らなくて壊れたと大騒ぎしてたらリモコンの電池が入ってませんでした. **チャンチャン**！ I was put out [I was pissed off] when I couldn't get my new TV to work. Turns out I forgot to put batteries in the controller! Heh-heh! That's all, folks! End of story!

チャンポン
◇酒とビールを**ちゃんぽん**に飲む drink sake and beer alternately [on the same occasion].
◇酒を**チャンポン**に飲む mix *one's* drinks.

ちょいワル slightly off; not quite good enough.
◇**ちょいワル**おやじ a roguishly fashionable older guy.

超…【ちょう…】
◇**超**ダサイ extremely [absolutely, totally] tacky.
◇**超**受ける⇨うける ★⇨くそ, げき…, ど…

調子こく【ちょうしこく】
◇**調子こい**てんじゃねえぞ（＝図に乗るな）. Don't push your luck (too far).; Don't get carried away.

ちょろい 〔簡単な〕easy; simple;〔口語〕a cinch; easy peasy;〔浅はかな〕(a bit) simple; (a bit) weak in the head.
◇**ちょろい**相手 an easy opponent.
◇そんなの**ちょろい**よ.〔口語〕It's a cinch [piece of cake, pushover].; It's as easy as pie.
◇こんな問題**ちょろい**, **ちょろい**. This question is a complete

cinch.
◇そんな**ちょろい**手にはひっかからないよ．I'm not going to fall for something that simple.; You don't fool me that easily.

チラ見する【チラみする】 take a (quick) glance; look out of the corner of *one's* eyes (at . . .).

ちらリズム the aesthetic of a sexy [tantalizing] glimpse; (the art of) giving a brief [tantalizing] glimpse [flash] (of *one's* underwear).

チンする 〔電子レンジで温める〕heat (up) . . . in a microwave; cook . . . in a microwave ★ microwave は「電子レンジ (microwave oven)」の短縮で，次のように動詞にもなる．
◇シチューを**チンする** microwave a stew; 〔口語〕nuke [zap] a stew.

チンタラ
◇**チンタラ**する dawdle; dillydally; goof off.
◇何を**チンタラ**やってるんだ．さっさとしろ．What are you doing dawdling like that? Get cracking.

つ

つーか，つうか，てゆうか【て言うか】 ..., or more precisely [exactly]; ..., or should I say.
◇海外旅行に行ったことがない．**つーか**行こうとも思わない． I've never been abroad; or perhaps I should say that I've no wish to go.

ツーショット
◇あこがれの俳優との**ツーショット** a photograph taken together with a favorite actor.
◇恋人と**ツーショット**で歩く walk alone with *one's* sweetheart.
◇彼と私の**ツーショット**の写真 a photograph of myself and my boyfriend.

ツートップ 〔サッカーで前線にフォワード 2 人を配置する攻撃態勢〕 a two-forward [two-striker] attack [formation].

使い倒す【つかいたおす】〔機能を徹底的に活用する〕apply all the functions (of a device). ★⇨…たおす
◇新作ソフトを**使い倒す** make full use of a new software.

突っ込み【つっこみ】〔漫才の〕the straight man. ★⇨ぼけ，あいかた
◇突っ込み担当だ play the straight man.
◇ストーリーに無理がありすぎて突っ込み所満載のドラマ a plot line so full of [so riddled with] inconsistencies that you don't know where to begin criticizing it.

ツッパリ
a (juvenile) delinquent;〔口語〕a punk; a tough (ie); a rowdy; a hoodlum; a hooligan.

美人局【つつもたせ】〔俗語〕a badger game; a scheme in which a man and a woman trick another man into a compromising situation and then blackmail him.
◇美人局をやる pull a badger game; carry out a blackmail scheme

つながり
◇京都つながりで（＝京都の話が出たついでに）今度は祇園祭の話題をお伝えします．While we're on the subject of Kyoto, here's some news about it's annual Gion Festival.

壷【つぼ】★⇨うける，あしつぼ
◇彼は人を笑わせるつぼを心得ている．He knows the essence of how to make people laugh.
◇この作品は娯楽映画のつぼを押さえている．This movie is exactly what an entertainment film should be.

つまみ食い【つまみぐい】
◇あの会社の社長は女性秘書のつまみ食いをするという噂だ．The rumour is that the president of that company is fooling around with his secretary.

つゆだく
✧つゆだくでお願いします．〔牛丼屋で〕
Plenty of sauce, please.

ヅラ 〔かつら〕a wig; a false head of hair;〔部分かつら〕a hairpiece; a switch; a toupee.
✧金髪のヅラ a blond(e) wig.
✧ヅラではげを隠す conceal [hide, cover over] a bald spot [*one's* baldness] with a wig [hairpiece, toupee].
✧ヅラをつける[かぶる] put on a wig [hairpiece, toupee]; wear a wig.
✧ヅラを取る take off a wig.
✧「あれはきっとヅラだよ」「ヅラじゃないでしょう」"I'll bet anything that's a wig." "I think it's his own hair."

釣りばか 【つりばか】 a fishing nut.

つるむ 〔口語〕hang around together (doing ...).
✧つるんで出かける tag along with ...
✧仲間とつるんで盛り場を歩き回る step out with friends to make the rounds of the entertainment district.

ツンデレ 〔最初はツンツンして冷淡だが後にデレデレと甘える〕be initially cool [aloof], but turn out to be clingy.

て

出会い【であい】
◇出会い系サイト an online dating site.
◇出会い(系)喫茶[カフェ] a dating cafe (where men pay to meet women).
◇幸せな出会い a happy [fortunate] encounter.
◇若者たちの出会いの場 a place where young people can meet.

Tバック【ティーバック】 a T-back (swimsuit [panty]); a thong.
★ thong は元来「ひも」の意だがよくこの意味で使う．

デカ 〔口語〕cop; dick. ★⇨サツ

手かざし(療法)【てかざし(りょうほう)】 pranic healing
★ pranic はインド哲学の「生気 (prana)」からの造語；(a) hand-healing therapy which avoids actual physical contact.

デカ盛り【デカもり】 an extra [a super] large portion.

テカり
◇顔のテカりをふせぐファンデーション a foundation cream that prevents facial shine.

出来ちゃった結婚【できちゃったけっこん】, 出来婚【できこん】 a marriage that results from an unplanned pregnancy; a marriage of necessity;〔特に未成年の女性が妊娠した場合〕a shotgun wedding [marriage] ★女性の父などが相手の男に責任を取らせるため，ショットガンで脅してでも結婚さ

せることから．⇨おめでたこん，さずかりこん

出来る【できる】

◇あの二人はできている．Those two are sleeping together [have a thing going on].

◇どうやら二人はできたらしい．Those two are evidently on intimate terms.

出来レース【できレース】 a fixed [rigged] race.

テクシー，テクる

◇テクシーで行く，テクる foot [〔俗語〕hoof] it; ride [go, come] on [by] shank's mare [pony].

◇テクって行こう．Let's foot [hoof] it.

デコ電【デコでん】〔デコレーションした携帯電話〕a bling phone [mobile]．★⇨キンキラ

デコトラ 〔電飾などでデコレーションしたトラック〕a truck gaudily decorated with chrome, air-brushed pictures and colored lights.

デコピン 〔指でおでこをはじくこと〕a finger flick to [on] the forehead.

✧…にデコピンをする give ... a finger flick to [on] the forehead.

デコる 〔デコレーションする〕decorate;〔口語〕bling (up). ★
⇨デコでん,デコトラ

デコルテ 〔肩を出す婦人服〕décolleté.
✧デコルテのガウン a décolleté [low-cut] gown.

デジタル万引き【デジタルまんびき】〔書店でカメラ付き携帯電話で情報を写し取ること〕"digital shoplifting"; taking digital photographs of publications in bookstores (without buying them).

…ですが何か【…ですがなにか】
✧ええ,40過ぎて独身でアニメおたくですが何か？ So, I'm past 40, unmarried, and an anime geek. Do you have a problem with that?

鉄子【てつこ】〔女性の鉄道ファン〕a trainspotter girl.

鉄ちゃん【てっちゃん】〔鉄道ファン〕a trainspotter;〔米〕a railroad buff [nerd];〔英〕a railway anorak.

徹夜組【てつやぐみ】〔チケットなどを入手するため前日から徹夜して並ぶ人々〕people who camp out (in line) overnight (for [to get] tickets).

デトックス 〔体内の毒素・老廃物排出を促進するという触れ込みの美容療法〕(a) detox.

デパガ,デパギャル 〔デパートの女性店員〕a department

store salesgirl.

デバカメ，出歯亀 ⇨のぞき

デパ地下【デパちか】〔デパートの地下の食料品・惣菜売場〕the food department in a department store basement.

手ブラ【てブラ】〔ブラジャーをはずし手や腕で胸を隠すポーズ〕hand bra.

でもしか…〔消極的動機による〕by default; for want of anything better (to do).
◇でもしか教師 a teacher by default.

出戻り【でもどり】a divorced woman (back at her parents' home); a divorcee. ★⇨バツイチ

てゆうか【て言うか】⇨つーか

デリケートゾーン a woman's delicate zone; the V-zone. ★Vは vagina から．⇨あそこがかゆい

デリヘル〔デリバリー・ヘルス〕a (massage parlor) call-girl service.

天然(ボケ)【てんねん(ボケ)】〔受けをねらっているわけではないのに言動がぼけていておかしいこと〕natural [inborn] dopiness [spaciness, stupidity];〔天然ボケの人〕〔口語〕a real space cadet [case]. ★ space cadet は元来「宇宙飛行の訓練生」のことで,「宙に浮いているようにぼんやりしたヤツ」を言う俗語．space case, spacy も同じ．

❖あいつちょっと**天然**入ってるよね．He's naturally a bit spacy, isn't he?
❖**天然**系の人 a naturally spacey character; a natural airhead.
❖**天然**パーマだ have natural curls [naturally curly hair].

テンパる
〔マージャンでテンパイ（あがり直前）になった時のように，せっぱ詰まって緊張する〕become [get] excited [flustered, worked up]; be about to explode (in anger).
❖年末はただでさえ忙しいのにパソコンが故障してすっかり**テンパ**ってしまった．I was already busy enough with the end of the year when my computer broke down and I flipped out.
❖仕事のストレスで**テンパ**っていたので，彼女の無神経な言葉についにキレてしまった．I was in a tizzy from all the stress at work, so her insensitive comment made me blow my top.

電ビラ【でんビラ】
〔電柱に貼りつける広告〕an advertisement on a 〔米〕utility [〔英〕telegraph] pole.

と

ど… 〔非常に〕very; immensely;〔ちょうど〕right; the very ...;〔ののしって〕damn; bloody;〔卑語〕fucking;〔強調して〕great. ★⇨げき…, ちょう…, くそ
◇どえらい人出 swarms [masses, a hell of a lot] of people.
◇どえらい金 a serious [humongous, stupendous] amount of money.
◇どえらいことをしでかす do something amazing [outstanding, stupendous].
◇その年, アメリカでどえらい事件が起こった. One hell of an incident happened in America that year.
◇どアップの写真 a full close-up (photograph); a photo(graph) in full close-up.
◇このどアホ！ You stupid bastard!;〔卑語〕You fucking idiot!
★⇨どこんじょう, どはくりょく, ストライク, エス

十一【といち】〔10日で1割の利息で金を貸すこと〕loaning money at 10 percent interest every 10 days; loans at the rate of 10 percent every 10 days;〔高利貸し〕a loan shark. ★⇨やみ

東京ドーム…杯分【とうきょうドーム…はいぶん】
◇1999年, 世界で消費されたビールの量は**東京ドーム**約107**杯分**である. In 1999 world consumption of beer was enough to fill Tokyo Dome roughly 107 times.

投稿【とうこう】
◇**投稿**する contribute; write; submit.
◇**投稿**写真[ビデオ, 動画] a submitted photograph [video].

◇(著作権のある作品の)違法**投稿** (an) illegal posting (of copyrighted material).
◇**投稿**サイト a contribution site.
◇動画**投稿**サイト a video sharing (Web) site.

盗撮 【とうさつ】
〔盗み撮り〕sneak [candid, unauthorized] photography; photography [shooting] with a hidden camera.
◇(有名人を)**盗撮**する take a sneak [an unauthorized] photo(graph) (of a celebrity).
◇**盗撮**写真 a sneak [a candid, an unauthorized] photo(graph); a candid camera photo [shot]; a secretly taken photograph [snap].
◇性的**盗撮** taking secret indecent photographs [videos] of women;〔スカート内の〕"upskirting."

どうよ？
◇夏の新作ドラマって**どうよ**？ Hey guys, what (do you think) about the new summer melodramas?

どS 【ドエス】, どM 【ドエム】 ⇨エス

トーシロー
〔しろうと〕an amateur; a nonprofessional; a layman; an ordinary person;〔初心者〕a novice;〔口語〕a greenhorn;〔門外漢〕an outsider.

トートバッグ
a tote bag.

ドカ食い 【ドカぐい】 ⇨むちゃぐい

ドカヘル〔作業用ヘルメット〕a hard hat.

ドカ弁【ドカベン】a packed meal in an outsize lunch-box.

独身貴族【どくしんきぞく】a well-off single [unattached] young man [woman]; a person who can live comfortably because he [she] is unmarried [single].

読モ【どくモ】, **読者モデル**【どくしゃモデル】a fashion model selected from among readers responding to a magazine recruitment campaign.

ど根性【どこんじょう】plenty [a lot] of guts; grit.

ドサ回り【ドサまわり】〔旅役者の一団〕a theatrical company on the road; a troupe of strolling actors and actresses;〔ドサ回りの劇団〕a barnstorming troupe;〔役者〕a barnstormer.
◇ドサ回りをする be on the road;〔口語〕barnstorm.

都市伝説【としでんせつ】 an urban legend.

ドス〔短刀〕a dagger; a dirk.
◇ドスを呑む wear a dagger in *one's* bosom.
◇ドスのきいた声で in a deep, threatening voice.
◇ドスをきかす threaten.

どストライク ⇨ストライク

ドタキャン〔どたん場でのキャンセル〕a last-minute cancellation.
◇ドタキャンする cancel ... at the last minute.

どっきり（カメラ）〔隠し撮り用カメラ〕candid camera;〔隠し撮り映像〕candid-camera footage.
◇衝撃のどっきり映像 a shocking image taken with a hidden camera.

どつく hit; strike; beat; punch; knock (down).
◇どついたろか. Do you want a thrashing?

ドッグイヤー〔犬の寿命が大体人間の七分の一なので，めまぐるしい情報化社会における七分の一年(約50日)を指す〕dog year.

父ちゃん坊や【とっちゃんぼうや】 a grown man who acts like a child [who has a childish side to him].

ドッチラケ a big turnoff; a major letdown.

トッポい
◇とっぽい服装の若者たち sharply dressed young people
◇とっぽいやつ a swaggerer.
◇新入りのくせにとっぽいやつだ．He's pretty cocky for a newcomer.

土手っ腹【どてっぱら】
◇…の土手っ腹に風穴をあける〔短刀で〕stab ...'s side (with a dagger);〔銃で〕drill holes in ...'s guts.

ど迫力【どはくりょく】
◇ど迫力の thrilling; gripping.
◇あの映画のカーアクションはど迫力だった．The car-chase scenes in that movie were rivetting.

ドバドバ，ドバッ
◇料理にソースをドバドバとかける pour gobs of sauce on *one's* food.

> **COLUMN**
>
> ## 日英の擬音語・擬態語 〜「びぎゃーっ！」は英語になるか？
>
> 同じ犬の鳴き声でも日本語では普通「ワンワン」だが英語では bow-wow が標準であるように，言葉によって擬音語や擬態語にも違いがある．一般的に言って日本語では漫画の発達もあり擬音語，擬態語の表現が英語よりも豊富で，漫画の英訳では擬音語・擬態語は無視あるいは簡略化されることが多い．例えば漫画「のだめカンタービレ」の「びぎゃーっ」という悲鳴は英訳版では単に aaah! や eeek!（きゃーっ，ひゃーっ）となっている．
>
> 漫画の英語翻訳では擬音語・擬態語を動詞で代用することも多く，例えば抜き足差し足で歩くシーンの「ソ〜」という擬態語は「こっそり歩く」という意味の動詞を用いて sneak，放心状態のシーンの「ぼーっ」は「ぼんやりする」という動詞 daze，あざ笑うシーンの「ニヤリ」は「にやにや笑う」を意味する sneer とするなどの例がある．
>
> また日本語のドカン→ドッカーンのような強調形は ker-, ka- のような接頭辞で示すことがある．例えば boom（ドーン，ズーン）に対し ker-boom（ドッカーン，ズドーン）のようなバリエーションができる．英語独特の表現もあり，たとえば日本のアニメや漫画でよく人に飛びついて抱きしめる「ぎゅむっ」「ヒシ」のような擬態語を glomp と表現する．
> ⇨がっぽり，がーん，ぎくっ，キンキラ，じゃじゃーん，ジュワーッと，チャンチャン，ピンポン，ブー

飛び込み【とびこみ】

◇飛び込み営業［セールス］cold selling; unsolicited sales activities.

◇飛び込みでセールスする make a cold [an unannounced] sales call.

◇飛び込み出産〔妊娠中一度も検診を受けず，陣痛が来てはじめて産科医を訪れて出産すること〕a "rush-in" [rushed] (hospital) birth.

◇飛び込み自殺 committing suicide by jumping in front of a [an on-rushing] train.

トホホ 〔弱々しい嘆き〕Oh, woe is me!
◇こんな**トホホ**なやつが相棒なんてついてないなあ！ It's just my bad luck to get stuck with such a pitiful guy [loser, sad sack] as my partner.

友達【ともだち】
◇**友達**感覚 a relationship like that of friends.
◇**友達**感覚で客に話しかける talk to customers as if they are friends.
◇**友達**夫婦〔友人感覚の夫婦〕a married couple who are (good [great]) pals with each other.

友チョコ【ともチョコ】〔バレンタインデーに女性の友人同士で贈りあうチョコレート〕chocolates exchanged by girls on Valentine's Day.

デコレートした友チョコの一例

とらばーゆ[トラバーユ]する change *one's* occupation [employment, profession, trade, job]; take up another employment; switch jobs.

トラ箱【トラばこ】〔警察の〕a sobering-up cell;〔米口語〕a drunk tank.

トリビア
〔雑学〕trivia;〔豆知識〕a snippet of knowledge; a handy piece of information.

ドル箱【ドルばこ】
a gold mine; a moneymaker;〔口語〕a money-spinner.
◇彼女はそのレコード会社の**ドル箱**だ．She is a gold mine for the record company.
◇**ドル箱**スター a star with high box-office value; a box-office star.
◇その路線はどの航空会社にとっても**ドル箱**である．That route is a moneymaker for every airline company (that flies it).
◇**ドル箱**路線〔航空路などの〕a moneymaking route;〔口語〕a cash-cow route.

トレーディング・カード，トレカ
〔収集・交換するスポーツ選手などの写真カード〕a trading card.

トレンディー
◇トレンディーな〔流行の先端を行く〕fashionable;〔流行に乗った〕trendy.
◇トレンディードラマ a fashion-driven television drama series.

ドロドロ
◇(人間関係が)ドロドロだ be in a murky, ugly state; be in a sordid state.
◇金や権力をめぐるドロドロした人間関係 human relations that have become sordid by struggles over money and power
◇ドロドロの愛欲生活 a sordid sexual life.
◇…の間のドロドロした愛憎 a love-hate struggle [battle, conflict] with [between] ….

泥縄(式)【どろなわ(しき)】

◇泥縄式でやる(＝泥棒を捕えて縄をなう) lock [close, shut] the stable [barn] door after the horse is stolen [has been stolen, has escaped]. ★「馬が盗まれた[逃げた]後で馬小屋に鍵をかける」を意味することわざ.

◇まさに泥縄もいいところだ. That is (an instance of) shutting the stable door after the horse is stolen.

◇泥縄式の対策 a countermeasure thrown together hastily (but too late).

◇泥縄式に at the eleventh hour. ★新約聖書「マタイ伝」に由来する「土壇場で」を意味する成句.

泥レス【どろレス】 mud wrestling.

ドロンする，ドロンをきめる abscond; take off; make off; disappear; pull the disappearing act.

ドン 〔マフィアなどのボス〕a don; a godfather.

◇政界のドン a political boss.

ドンケツ，ドン尻【どんじり】 the tail [tag] end;〔人・チームなど〕a tailender;〔最下位〕the lowest rank; the very bottom.

◇ドン尻に at the end [bottom]; at the very last;〔競技で〕in the cellar.

◇ドン尻のチーム the cellar-dwelling team; the tailender(s).

トンズラ (a) flight; escape.
◇トンズラする［こく］run away; flee; escape; decamp; make *one's* escape［〔口語〕getaway］;〔口語〕lam;〔口語〕beat［hook, hightail］it;〔俗語〕skedaddle; scarper; take it on the lam; do a bunk［runner］.

トンデモ本【トンデモぼん】a sensationalistic［an absurd, an outrageous］book.

ドンパチ〔戦争〕a war; a battle;〔武力抗争〕a shootout.

ドン引き【ドンびき】
◇彼女の涙ながらの弁解に一座は**ドン引き**だった．Her tearful excuses made everyone terribly uncomfortable［produced an extremely awkward atmosphere］.

ドンピシャ(リ)
◇ドンピシャのタイミングで with perfect timing.
◇どんぴしゃりな［の］答え an answer that hits the nail on the head.
◇どんぴしゃりである be right on the nose; hit the mark［the nail on the head］;〔答えが〕be exactly［quite］right; be quite to the point; really hit the bull's-eye; be spot-on;〔…に適合している〕fit［suit］...to a T［tee］;〔計算などが〕be perfectly correct.
◇実験の結果は予想と**どんぴしゃり**だった．The results of the experiment were exactly as predicted.

ドンマイ〔Don't mind.（気にするな）から〕Never mind.; Don't let it bother you.

な

なあなあ
✧**なあなあ**で済ます let ... by without comment; pretend not to notice; not make a fuss.
✧…と**なあなあ**でやっていく get along on a live-and-let-live basis with ....
✧彼らは仲間の失敗を**なあなあ**で済ませた．They winked at [did nothing about] their colleague's blunder.; They allowed the mistake of their colleague to pass without comment.

ナイス・バディ ★⇨ボン・キュッ・ボン
✧彼女は**ナイス・バディ**だ．She is sexy [voluptuous].; She has a lovely [nice] body.
✧おーっ，**ナイス・バディ**！ Wow! Nice body!; Wow! Sexy!

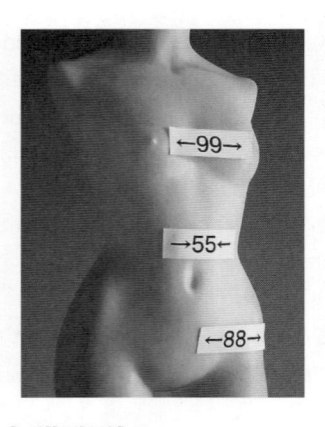

内臓脂肪【ないぞうしぼう】 visceral fat.
✧**内臓脂肪**型肥満 visceral obesity.

ナイン ⇨ひんにゅう

ナウい fashionable; stylish;〔口語〕(very) with it; hip; groovy; be in; be the in thing. ★⇨ださい

萎え(る)【なえ(る)】〔性的不能になる〕become impotent; be unable to get an erection;〔興冷め, 失望, 幻滅〕a loss of interest; a letdown feeling; disgust; dislike; disappointment. ★⇨もえ
◇明日は休日出勤しろだって．激**萎え**だあ．Tomorrow I have to go to work on what was supposed to be my day off. What a drag [Major bummer]!
◇**萎え**要素 a disappointing feature [characteristic].
◇あのゲームの下手な効果音は**萎え**要素だ．That game's lousy sound effects are a real turnoff.

中食【なかしょく】〔持ち帰り食・惣菜〕(a) home meal replacement (略: HMR).

中抜けする【なかぬけする】take a little time off (work); step [pop] out (and come right back).
◇仕事を**中抜け**して歯医者に行った．I took some time off work [I left work for a while] to go to the dentist.

仲良しクラブ[グループ]【なかよしクラブ[グループ]】〔馴れ合い集団〕a chummy [pally] group; (a group of) good pals.
◇**仲良しクラブ**では試合には勝てない．チームのメンバーが互いに競い合うようでなくてはだめだ．Just being good pals [chummy (with each other)] won't win games. You've got to compete (with each other).

ながら
◇**ながら**勉強 studying while watching TV or listening to the radio.
◇**ながら**族 those who work or study while listening to the radio or watching TV.
◇テレビをつけっ放しの**ながら**食い eating while watching TV.
◇〔テレビ・ラジオの〕**ながら**視聴 watching TV [listening to the radio] while doing something else [engaged in another activity].

何か？【なにか】 ⇨ …ですがなにか

何が悲しくて【なにがかなしくて】
◇**何が悲しくて**(＝何の因果で，いったいどうして)こんな本を買っちゃったのやら．What in the world made me buy this book?; Why in (all) hell did I buy this book anyway.; Why did I ever buy this book in the first place?

何気に【なにげに】
〔意図せず〕unintentionally; without intending to do so;〔ふと〕casually; accidentally; by accident;〔不注意に〕carelessly; inadvertently; unguardedly;〔さりげなく〕as if nothing had happened; unconcernedly;〔何も気づかず〕innocently;〔けっこう，意外に〕surprisingly; pretty.
◇彼女**何気に**強引なところあるね．She can (sometimes) be pretty bossy, can't she?; At times she can be sort of bossy, can't she?
◇あの人若く見えるけど**何気に**先輩でした．He looks young but actually [in fact] he's even older than I am.
◇疲れたと言いつつ**何気に**議論に参加してますが．Though I say I'm tired I'm still somehow in the discussion, you see.

鍋奉行【なべぶぎょう】
a person who directs the cooking of the food in a pot on a table; a pot boss.

ナマ足，生脚【なまあし】 bare legs.

舐める【なめる，ナメる】〔馬鹿にする，あなどる〕treat ... like a fool; disparage; make light of ... ; hold ... cheap [in contempt]; look down on ... ;〔ゆっくりとパン撮影する〕pan slowly; do a slow pan;〔手前の人[物]越しに撮影する〕film [shoot] over ... 's shoulder [with ... in the foreground].
　◇初めから相手を**なめて**かかる regard *one's* opponent with contempt from the outset; hold *one's* opponent lightly from the start.
　◇**なめた**態度を取る take a contemptuous [disparaging] attitude
　◇**なめた**口をきく speak in a tone of disparagement.
　◇素人だと思って**なめる**なよ．Don't look down your nose at me because you think I'm an amateur.
　◇**なめて**かかると痛い目にあうぞ．If you take it [him] lightly, you're going to wind up getting burned [being sorry].
　◇てめえ，**なめてん**のか？ Are you making a fool of me?
　◇**なめた**まねをしやがって．You think you can make a fool of me!

成田離婚【なりたりこん】 a Narita divorce; divorce on returning from *one's* honeymoon.

なるはや〔なるべく早く〕ASAP ★ as soon as possible の略．
　◇**なるはや**で返事ください．Please reply at your earliest convenience.; Please let me have your answer as soon as possible [ASAP, asap].

なるへそ I see; it is true; indeed; really; well (yes); as you say;〔確かに〕(to be) sure.

なんだかんだ【何だかんだ】

◇何だかんだ(と)言って〔偽りの口実で〕on one [some] pretext or another;〔いろいろな理由で〕for one [some] reason or another

◇何だかんだ(と)言っている間にもう着いてしまった． As we were talking about this and that, we found ourselves arriving at our destination.

◇彼は何だかんだ(と)言い訳ばかりしていて一向に着手してくれない． He's always making excuses and never gets around to working.

◇何だかんだで金がいる． I need money for this and that.

◇何だかんだと忙しい． I am busy with one thing and another.

◇このところ何だかんだ(と)物入りが続いて懐が苦しい． With all these expenses, I'm strapped for cash these days.

◇何だかんだ言っても彼女は夫を愛してるんだよ． Whatever [In spite of everything, Regardless of what] she says, she loves her husband.

なんちゃって，なんつって

◇君は僕の太陽だ，なんちゃって． You are like the sun for me. Oh God, how corny!

◇愛は地球を救う，なんつって． Love will save the world. Hey, did I say that?

◇そう，あの人が好きなの…なーんちゃって！ Yes, I love him. *Not*!

◇なんちゃって女子高生〔女子高生になりすましているニセモノ〕a girl who pretends to be a high school student; a fake [phony] high school girl.

◇なんちゃって制服〔生徒でない人が着ている学校の制服〕a school uniform worn by a nonstudent; a faux school uniform.

何でもあり【なんでもあり】 no holds barred ★元レスリング用語で，「どんな決め技（hold）も禁止（bar）されない」の意; no limits.

◇この国の選挙は誹謗中傷贈収賄**何でもあり**だ．The elections in this country are rife with slander, libel, and bribery, whatever it takes to win.

◇このスポーツは観客を喜ばせるためなら**何でもあり**だ．In this sport, they do whatever they have to in order to please the spectators.

◇Anything goes here. ここでは**何でもあり**だ．

ナンパ［軟派］（する） approach; address; buttonhole;〔口語〕chat up;〔特に性交を目的として〕pick up. ★⇨ぎゃくナン，おもちかえり

◇街で若い女性を**ナンパする** approach [buttonhole] a young woman on the street (and invite her for a drink); chat up a girl on the street.

◇「どうやって今の彼と知り合ったの？」「喫茶店で**ナンパされた**の」"How did you meet your current boyfriend?" "He asked me for a date [chatted me up] in a coffee shop."

◇初めて街で**ナンパ**にあってこわいようなうれしいような気がした．The first time a man approached me [tried to chat me up] on the street I was both scared and delighted.

◇5人めで**ナンパ**に成功した．On his fifth attempt, he finally talked a woman into a date [persuaded a woman to go out with him].

なんぼ

◇芸能界はしょせん売れて**なんぼ**の世界だ．In the entertainment world, it's all a matter of how popular you are.

に

ニーソ ⇨オーバーニー

ニート 〔職業を持たず，就学中でもなく，職業訓練を受けているわけでもない人〕a NEET. ★ NEET は "not in employment, education or training" の略.
◇生活保護ニート a NEET receiving livelihood protection; a welfare NEET.

ニケツ【にケツ】〔二人乗り〕★⇨さんケツ
◇ニケツする ride together [double, in tandem].

ニコイチ，二個一 〔2台の機器，特に車の各々から使える部品を寄せ集めて1台に復元すること〕restoring (a car) from parts taken from it and another; cannibalizing (a car) for parts for another.

二号【にごう】a mistress; a kept woman.
◇二号を置く[囲う] take [keep] a mistress.

2次元キャラ【にじげんキャラ】character in a manga book or an anime video.

二八【にっぱち】〔商取引が不活発とされる2月と8月〕February and August (when business is supposed to be sluggish); the sluggish months of February and August.

二刀流【にとうりゅう】⇨バイ

二枚目【にまいめ】〔ハンサムな役柄〕the role of a lover [beau]; a lover's part; 〔二枚目役者〕a beau-part actor; 〔ハンサム〕a handsome [good-looking] man. ★⇨イケメン
✧二枚目半 a comedian in a lover's part.

ニャンニャン ⇨エッチ(する)

ニューハーフ a drag queen; 〔卑語〕a shemale.

ぬ

抜く【ぬく】 ⇨せんずり，いく
♦...の顔を**抜く**(＝アップで撮る)show ...'s face in close-up; show ... full-face.

脱ぐ【ぬぐ】
♦あの女優が**脱いだ**とは驚きだ．It surprises me that that actress should strip for the camera.
♦ユニフォームを**脱ぐ** take off *one's* uniform;〔選手が現役を引退する〕retire (from playing).
♦彼はプロ野球のユニフォームを**脱いだ**．He put on his pro baseball uniform for the last time. ★「最後の試合のために着た」の意．

濡れ落ち葉【ぬれおちば】〔妻にくっついて離れない退職後の男〕a (newly) retired man who gets underfoot at home.

ね

ネアカ, 根明 an innately cheerful person; a happy-go-lucky person; a natural optimist.

ねぎだく
◇ねぎだくでお願いします.〔牛丼屋で〕Extra onions, please.
★⇨つゆだく

ネクラ, 根暗 a congenitally gloomy person.

猫まんま【ねこまんま】, 猫飯【ねこめし】〔ご飯にけずり節をのせ, みそ汁か少量の醤油をかけただけの簡単な食事〕boiled rice and dried bonito flakes with miso soup or a few drops of soy sauce poured on it.

猫耳, ネコミミ〔猫の耳をつけた美少女キャラ〕catgirl;〔仮装用の〕cat ears.

値ごろ【ねごろ】〔妥当な値段〕a reasonable [a moderate, an affordable] price.
◇値ごろである be reasonable [moderate] in price; be affordable.
◇だいたいこの辺が値ごろかな．This is just about the right price range.
◇値ごろ感のある住みよさそうなマンションが見つかった．I found an apartment that looks comfortable and feels affordable.

ねじれ国会【ねじれこっかい】
◇ねじれ国会のため政府は法案を通せないでいる．Because the two houses of the Diet are at loggerheads, the Government has been unable to pass new laws. ★ at loggerheads は「対立して」の意．

ネズミ捕り【ネズミとり】〔警察のスピード違反取り締まり〕a speed trap; a radar trap.
◇ネズミ捕りにひっかかる be caught in a speed trap.

ネタ
◇ネタ帳〔お笑い芸人がネタを書き留めたり検討したりするためのノート〕an idea [a brainstorming] notebook.
◇ネタばれ〔結末などをばらす記述〕a (movie[story]) spoiler.
◇ネタばれは禁止です．No spoilers [spoiling], please.
◇ネタばれ注意．〔この先には物語の結末などが書かれているので注意，という警告文〕Spoiler Warning.

ネット
◇ネットアイドル an Internet [online] idol [star].
◇ネットいじめ〔インターネットサイトへの誹謗中傷の書き込みによるいじめ〕cyberbullying; net bullying;〔ネット上の中傷〕(a) slander [libel] on the Net.

◇ネット依存症 Internet addiction disorder（略: IAD）.
◇ネット中毒 Internet addiction.
◇ネット中毒者 a net-head［Net-head］; a netaholic［Netaholic］.
◇ネット占い online fortune-telling.
◇ネット競売［オークション］サイト an Internet auction site; a Net auction site.
◇ネットギャンブル a Net gambling.
◇ネット詐欺〔インターネット上の〕(an) Internet fraud; an Internet scam.
◇ネット(集団)自殺 an Internet suicide pact.
◇ネットカフェ an Internet café.
◇ネットカフェ難民〔住む場所がなく日雇い仕事で生計を立てながら終夜営業のインターネットカフェや漫画喫茶などで夜を明かす人〕an Internet café refugee; a homeless person who spends the night［seeks asylum］at Internet cafés.

ネルドリップ〔フランネルのフィルターを使うコーヒーのドリップ方式〕flannel drip (coffee); the flannel drip method.

ねんね〔年の割に世間知らずで幼稚な娘〕a baby; an innocent; an ingenuous girl.
◇うちの娘はまだ**ねんね**です．Our daughter still acts like a baby.

の

能[脳]天気な【のうてんきな】laid-back; lightweight; happy-go-lucky; easygoing.

脳トレ【のうトレ】〔脳力トレーニング〕brain training.

ノーギャラ
◇ノーギャラでコマーシャルに出演する appear in a commercial free [without being paid].
◇ノーギャラの仕事 non-paying [unpaid] jobs.

ノーパン
◇ノーパンで with no underwear (on); not wearing panties.
◇ノーパン喫茶 a tea house where the waitresses wear short skirts and no underwear.

ノーブラ
◇ノーブラの braless; not wearing a brassiere.
◇彼女はいつもノーブラだ．She never wears a bra.

ノーヘル
◇ノーヘルの without (wearing) a helmet.
◇ノーヘルでバイクに乗っていて警官に止められた．He was stopped by a policeman for riding [when he was riding] a motorcycle without a helmet on [without wearing a helmet].

のぞき，のぞく ★⇨とうさつ
◇女の裸をのぞく peep at a naked woman.

✧のぞき部屋 a peep-show room.
✧のぞき屋［魔］a voyeur; a peeping Tom. ★ peeping Tom（のぞき屋トム）はイギリスの伝説上の人物．ある貴婦人が町民を苦しめる重税をなくしてもらう交換条件として素っ裸で町中を通った時，町民は全員家に閉じこもって見なかったが，ただ一人トムという男がのぞき見て天罰で目が潰れたという．日本語でのぞき屋を「出歯亀（でばかめ）」とも言うが，これは明治時代にのぞき行為や殺人を犯した男が出っ歯で池田亀太郎という名だったことから．
✧のぞき見をしてここにぶちこまれたのさ．I've been put in here for voyeurism [for being a peeping Tom].

COLUMN

英語の名前あれこれ

上記「出歯亀」のように人名が普通の単語となったものを英語でエポニム（eponym）と呼ぶ．日本でなじみの深いものには「サンドイッチ（Sandwich; 最初に考案した英国貴族）」「ボイコット（Boycott; アイルランドで住民から村八分にあった土地管理人）」「バーボン（Bourbon; 米国の醸造地の名だが，元来はフランスの「ブルボン王家」にちなむ地名）」「グッピー（Guppy; 魚類研究者の名）」「ブルマー（Bloomer; 米国の女権活動家で，スカートでない活動的な服を提唱したことから，元来は女性用スラックスなどを指した）」などがあるが，必ずしも英語と一致するとは限らない．たとえば「ホッチキス」は発明者の名だが，英語では「ステイプラー（stapler）」「U字型針（staple）で綴じる器具）と言わないと通じない．また「リンチ（lynch）」も米国の裁判官の名から来ているが，英語では「集団で不法に（特に絞首刑で）処刑する」の意味が普通．

英語の人名にも当然種々のイメージや流行がある．例えばある調査ではAndrew（誠実だが未熟），Dennis（不器用），Donald（人当たりが良い），Richard（ハンサム），Robert（内気），Nancy（意地悪），Sally（子供っぽい）などのイメージが見られるという．最近の英語圏で人気がある名前は男はJacob, Jack, Michaelなど，女はEmma, Emily, Sophiaなどが多い．変わったところでは米国のテレビ番組で紹介されたことか

> ら人気を呼んだ Nevaeh（ネヴェイヤ；heaven（天国）の逆書き）がある．姓名判断は画数の代わりにアルファベットを数字に置き換えてその合計数で占うのが普通．
> また非英語圏にルーツを持つ人はそれぞれの母国語に由来する名前も珍しくない．実父がケニア人だったオバマ米大統領のフルネーム Barack Hussein Obama のうち，Barack はアラビア語で「恵まれた」，Hussein は同じく「良い，美しい，立派な」を意味し，イラクのフセイン元大統領と同じだが，イスラム文化圏では日本の「良男」「良太」のようにごくありふれた名前である．

ノってる，乗ってる

◇みんな，**ノってる**か．Are you into it [high]? ★⇨ノリノリ
◇彼女は今乗りに**乗っている**．She's on top of the world.

飲み会【のみかい】
a drinking party [bout]．★⇨コンパ

飲み放題【のみほうだい】
drinking as much as one wants；〔掲示で「お代わり自由」〕free refills．★喫茶店などのお代わり自由のコーヒーなどを bottomless cup（底無しのカップ）と呼ぶことがある．

◇酒は**飲み放題**です．You can drink all you want.
◇今晩は**飲み放題**だ．We can drink as much as we want tonight.
◇ビール 3,000 円で**飲み放題**．〔掲示〕All the beer you can drink for ¥3,000.

ノミ屋【ノミや】
〔競馬などの違法な私設の賭け屋〕an illegal bookmaker [〔口語〕bookie].

ノリノリ ★⇨ノってる

◇客は 1 曲目から**ノリノリ**だった．The audience was really into it right from the first song.

ノンケ，ノン気〔同性愛嗜好がない人〕a straight man; a straight arrow;〔ノンケの人たちをまとめて〕straights.
✧一見ゲイ風だが彼は**ノン気**だ． He looks gay but he's really straight.

は

バーコードヘア 〔ハゲ隠しのすだれ頭〕a combover.
★薄くなった頭髪をむりやり櫛 (comb) でなでつけることから.

パーッと, ぱあっと
◇飲み屋でパーッとやる carouse at a bar; have a drink and have fun.
◇彼女は宝くじで当たった金をぱあっと使ってしまった. She went through all of the lottery money she won in no time.

バイ(セクシュアル)
◇彼はバイ[二刀流]だ. He is bisexual [〔口語〕bi].

ハイテンションの　high-strung; worked-up; intense; frantic.

ハイレグ　high-cut (leg); high cut.
◇ハイレグの水着 a swimsuit with high cut legs; a high cut bathing suit [swimsuit].
◇ハイレグのビキニ a high cut bikini.
◇ハイレグカット high leg cut.

馬鹿受け【ばかうけ】⇨うける

バカスカ ⇨がっぽり

バカップル〔ばかなカップル〕a "foolish couple"; a couple who smooch or fondle each other in a public place.

ハグする hug . . . ; give . . . a hug.

爆睡する【ばくすいする】sleep like a log. ★「倒れた丸太 (log) のように，起きることなく眠る」の意．同様にこま (top) が回り終えると倒れることから sleep like a top とも言う．

爆弾【ばくだん】
◇肩に**爆弾**を抱えている投手 a pitcher whose shoulder could go at any moment.
◇**爆弾**発言をする drop a bombshell; make a bombshell announcement.
◇**爆弾**犯人，**爆弾**魔 a bomber. ★⇨じばくテロ

バク転【バクてん】, バック転【バックてん】 a backward somersault [hand-spring].

バクバク 〔胸の高鳴り〕pounding; throbbing.
◇…の胸がバクバクする *one's* heart goes pitter-patter [pit-a-pat].

爆発ヘア【ばくはつヘア】 explosive [unruly] hair.

白馬の王子【はくばのおうじ】 ⇨おうじさま

パクる, パクり
◇文章をパクる crib a paragraph.
◇アイデアをパクる lift an idea.
◇〔犯人を〕パクる arrest; round up; nab.
◇現行犯でパクられる be nabbed in the act.
◇彼の新曲はアメリカで流行った歌のパクりだそうだ. There are rumors that he pirated a song popular in America for his new tune.

バグる become [get, act] buggy; act up; behave strangely.
◇今日は朝からコンピューターがバグって仕事にならない. My computer has been acting up [on the fritz] since this morning and I haven't been able to do any work.

化ける【ばける】 ⇨おおばけ

箱買い【はこがい】 buying [purchasing] ... by the box [in bulk]; bulk purchasing.

ハコ乗りする，箱乗りする【はこのりする】 ride in a car head and shoulders out the window.

ハジキ ⇨チャカ

梯子【はしご】 a ladder.
◇はしごが外される〔孤立する〕be left high and dry.
◇人を二階に上げてはしごを外すようなことはしないでくれよ．Surely you're not going to build me up like that and then pull the rug from under my feet [leave me to fend for myself]?
◇〔飲み屋を〕3軒ハシゴする go drinking at three bars (in succession).

パシリ 〔使い走り〕
◇上級生のパシリをやらされる be made to run errands for *one's* seniors.

ハズイ 〔恥ずかしい〕
◇面と向かって「愛してる」なんてハズくて言えるかよ．I'd be too embarrassed to just say "I love you" straight to her face.

はずす ⇨すべる

バタンキュー
◇枕に頭をのせたとたんにバタンキューで眠ってしまう drop off (to sleep) as soon as *one's* head hits the pillow.
◇とても疲れていたので，その日はバタンキューと寝てしまった．It was an exhausting day and I was out like a light as soon as I pulled up the covers.
◇このところ毎日バタンキューなので手紙を書く暇もない．These days I've been falling into bed as soon as I get home, so I haven't

even had time to write a letter.

ハチ公【ハチこう】 "Hachi," the faithful dog; a dog, Hachi, who continued to wait outside Shibuya Station every day for his master, Tokyo University Professor Ueno Hidesaburo, for 10 years after Ueno's death in 1925.
◇忠犬**ハチ公**像 the statue of (the faithful dog) Hachi(ko) (outside Shibuya Station).
◇**ハチ公**前広場 the square in front of the Hachiko statue (at Shibuya Station).
◇それじゃあ，12時に**ハチ公**前でね．Okay, see you at twelve o'clock in front of Hachiko [of the Hachiko statue].

パチモン 〔ブランド製品の偽物〕 a counterfeit product; an imitation;〔俗語〕a knockoff.

ハチャメチャ ⇨めちゃくちゃ

バツイチ (the state of being) once-divorced. ★⇨こぶつき
◇**バツイチ**同士のカップル a couple, both of whom have been divorced (once); a couple, each with a divorce behind them.
◇**バツイチ**の人 somebody who has had one divorce; a once-divorced person.
◇私**バツイチ**です．I've been married once (but now I'm divorced).

パツキン 〔金髪(女)〕 a blonde (woman).

バック転【バックてん】 ⇨バクてん

バックレる 〔しらばっくれる〕 pretend not to know; feign [affect] ignorance; play innocent;〔逃げる；さぼる〕evade; play truant.
◇授業をバックレる cut class.

罰ゲーム【ばつゲーム】 a punishment; a penalty. ★⇨ NG（エヌジー）ワード

初体験【はつたいけん】，初エッチ【はつエッチ】 ⇨チェリーボーイ，ふでおろし

バッタ
◇バッタ物（もん）〔不正規ルートの安値商品〕goods sold off through irregular channels at very low prices [a loss].
◇バッタ屋 a seller of [dealer in] irregular, low-priced goods.

バッチグー (absolutely) perfect.
◇バッチグーなタイミング perfect timing
◇最後にバジルの葉をのせて，これで味も香りもバッチグーだ．Top it off with some basil leaves and it will taste and smell absolutely perfect.

発展場【ハッテンば】〔ゲイが集まる場所〕a (gay) cruising site [place]; a gay venue.

ぱっと見【ぱっとみ】
◇このデザインはぱっと見はいいが，よく見ると雑だ．The design looks interesting at a first glance but it doesn't stand up to closer scrutiny.

ハッパ，葉っぱ 〔大麻〕grass; weed. ★米国の俗語で 420

(four twenty) とも言う．一説ではある高校の生徒が毎日午後4時20分に集まって吸っていたことから．

ハデ婚, 派手婚【はでこん】a big [flashy, 〔口語〕blow-out] wedding. ★⇨じみこん

鼻【はな】
◇鼻ぺちゃだ have a flat [pug] nose.
◇鼻ぺちゃな顔 a pug-nosed [flat-nosed] face.
◇赤ちゃんが鼻ちょうちんを出した．The baby blew a little bubble from its nose.
◇彼は鼻ちょうちんを出して(＝のんきに)寝ていた．He was snoring away.; He was in (a) profound slumber.; He was lost to the world.
◇鼻うがい nasal irrigation (by inhaling fluid into the nose and expelling it out the mouth).

花丸【はなまる】a circle adorned with petals (to indicate "very good" on a test paper). ★⇨あかまるきゅうじょうしょう

パニクる lose *one's* head; (get into a) panic. ★英語の panic はしばしば「あわてる，パニックになる」という動詞として使う．
◇突然お祝いのスピーチをしろと言われて完全にパニクった．I was quite flustered when I was suddenly called on to give a congratulatory speech. ★⇨テンパる

パネエ ⇨はんぱない

ババシャツ a long-sleeved thermal undershirt.

ハブ(る) 〔のけ者・仲間はずれにする；村八分の短縮〕leave ... out (in the cold); ignore; put ... on one side; exclude; shun; keep clear of ...; blackball.
◇ハブにされる be treated as an outcast [like a pariah].
◇ハブられて話に入れなかった．They kept me out of their conversation completely.; They ignored me and wouldn't let me join in the conversation.

バブリーな 〔バブルの時代のような発想の；金づかいが荒い〕extravagant; ostentatious.
◇バブリーな施設 an overly [excessively] expensive [extravagant, luxurious] facility.

バブル a bubble (economy).
◇バブルがはじけて地価が暴落した．The economic bubble burst and land prices plummeted.
◇バブルの崩壊 the collapse of the bubble economy.

はまる 〔…に夢中になる，のめり込む〕be mad [crazy] about ...; be hooked on ...;〔口語〕be (heavily) into .... ★⇨つぼ，うける
◇ロックにどっぷりはまっている be (heavily) into rock music.
◇ジャズにはまる be crazy about jazz.
◇私が囲碁にはまったきっかけ what got me hooked on go.
◇彼は草野球の楽しさにすっかりはまっている．He's completely sold on the joys of sandlot baseball.

ハモる 〔…とハーモニーで歌う〕harmonize [sing harmony] (with ...).

早押しクイズ【はやおしクイズ】a push-button quiz.

早弁【はやべん】eating *one's* packed lunch [bent] before the midday break.

パラサイトシングル〔成人・就職後も親元で暮らす未婚者〕unmarried young adults who continue living with their parents in order to save on rent and avoid doing housework; parasitic singles.

バラドル a TV idol who appears mainly on variety shows.

パラパラ〔ユーロビートに合わせて手を動かす日本のディスコダンス〕para para; disco dancing with synchronized arm motions. ◇〔ページを素早く次々にめくるとアニメのように動いて見える〕パラパラ漫画 flip animation; a flipbook.

ばらまき
　◇ばらまき政治 pork-barrel politics.
　◇ばらまき予算 a shotgun budget.
　◇ばらまき公共事業 public works pork-barrel projects [pork].
　◇ばらまき福祉 subsidizing welfare recklessly and indiscriminately; throwing money at social problems.

はらみ婚【はらみこん】⇨できちゃったけっこん

バリ3【バリさん】〔携帯の電波が一番いい状態〕optimal [the best] reception;〔そのマーク〕three (reception) bars. ★外国の携帯はこの「アンテナ」が5本のものも多く見られ, "I have five bars."(アンテナが5本立ってる) のように言うこともある. ⇨ケータイ, けんがい

ハリセン，張り扇
a large pleated paper fan designed to produce maximum noise, used by traditional storytellers to provide accompaniment and gesture and also, in various Japanese comedies, as a mock weapon for whacking people on the head.

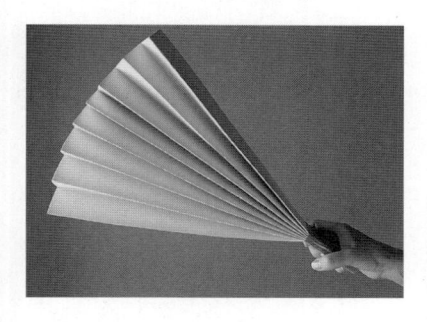

バレバレ
〔見え透いた〕immediately seen through;〔一目瞭然の〕obvious (at a glance).
◇「なんでウソだってわかった？」「だってバレバレだもん！」 "How did you know it was a lie?" "It was obvious!"
◇君はウソをつくとまばたきする癖があるだろ．バレバレだよ．Whenever you lie, you blink your eyes. It's a dead giveaway.
◇バレバレのウソ a transparent [an obvious] lie; a manifest [palpable] lie.
◇あいつの魂胆(こんたん)はバレバレだ．His intentions are obvious.; His motive is apparent.

パワー全開【パワーぜんかい】
◇パワー全開で at full throttle; at maximum power.
◇これを読めばあなたも明日から**パワー全開**．If you read this book you'll be using your power to the full from tomorrow!
◇今年も**パワー全開**でいこう．Let's really go at it [give it everything we've got] this year, too.

パワハラ，パワーハラスメント〔職権をかさに着たいやがらせ〕power harassment; using *one's* power [position] to harass [bully] subordinates;〔職場でのいやがらせ全般〕workplace harassment. ★⇨セクハラ，ブラハラ

半…【はん…】
◇半ライス[ラーメン，チャーハン] a half serving of rice [ramen, fried rice].

半ライス　　　　　半身浴

半身浴【はんしんよく】a hip bath.

番宣【ばんせん】〔番組宣伝〕a program announcement [promotion].

パンダ
◇客寄せパンダ an event [person] to attract people [customers]; an attraction; a draw.
◇パンダ目(め)〔マスカラが崩れて目のまわりが黒くなる状態〕mascara circles [rings] under *one's* eyes; mascara-smeared [mascara-smudged] eyes; panda eyes.

パンチドランカー〔格闘技，特にボクシングで脳に損傷を

受けた人〕a punch-drunk boxer. ★英語では普通 punch drunker という表現はしない．パンチドランカーの脳機能障害は次のように呼ばれる．dementia pugilistica（略：DP）; boxer's dementia; punch-drunk syndrome.

半チャーハン【はんチャーハン】, 半チャン ⇨はん…

パンチラ
◇パンチラ写真 a panty shot (picture). ★⇨とうさつ

はんなり〔落ち着いた華やかさ〕
◇はんなりしたおなごはん a serene, elegant girl.
◇はんなりと踊る dance in a self-possessed and elegant manner.
◇はんなりとした味 a restrained but lively taste.

半端(じゃ)ない【はんぱ(じゃ)ない】, ハンパねえ 〔ものすごい〕immense; enormous; tremendous; awful; terrible;〔すばらしい〕superb; wonderful; amazing;〔口語〕great; fantastic; terrific; awesome.
◇彼の食べ物に対するこだわりは半端じゃなかった．He was incredibly fussy about his food.; His fussiness about food had to be seen to be believed.
◇怖さハンパねえぞ，この映画！ That movie's really scary!
◇半端なくうれしい be awfully glad; be immensely pleased.
◇半端なく腹が減った．I'm incredibly hungry.; I'm absolutely starving.

パンピー〔一般の人（ピープル）〕ordinary people.

半ライス【はんライス】, 半ラーメン【はんラーメン】
⇨はん…

韓流【はんりゅう】
◇**韓流**スター a Korean movie star.
◇**韓流**ブーム a Korean boom [fad].
◇わが国の**韓流**ブームは一向に衰える気配がない．Our country's fad for all things Korean shows no sign of waning.

ひ

ピー 〔発信音などの〕a beep; a bleep.
◇ピー(という音)を入れて言葉を消す〔放送で〕bleep a word (out). ★⇨ほうそうきんしようご
◇おかけ直しいただくか，ピーッという発信音のあとにメッセージをお願いします．〔留守番電話のメッセージ〕Please call later, or leave a message after the beep [tone].

ピーカン 〔撮影用語で，快晴の意〕
◇今日はピーカンだ．Today's fine (for filming).

B級【ビーきゅう】
◇B級映画 a B movie; a grade-B [B-grade] movie.
◇B級グルメ a semi-gourmet; a gourmet on the cheap.

ピーポー(パーポー) 〔サイレンの音〕the "bee-po" sound of an ambulance siren.

ヒール 〔プロレスなどの悪役・憎まれ役〕bad guy;〔俗語〕heel;〔憎まれ役〕the man you love to hate.
◇ヒールを演じる play the villain's role.

ビールかけ 〔祝勝会での〕a celebratory beer shower.
◇ビールかけをする shower each other with beer.

日帰り温泉【ひがえりおんせん】 a hot spring (bath) for day trippers [guests not staying overnight].
◇日帰り温泉施設 a hot spring bathing facility for day trippers.

ぴかぴか
✧ピカピカの一年生 a brand-new first grader [first year student].

引きこもり【ひきこもり】 withdrawal into oneself [from society]; social withdrawal; going into seclusion; shunning [avoiding] other people (to a pathological extent).
✧引きこもりの若者 a young man who goes into seclusion [refuses to go out (into the world)].
✧引きこもりをやめる stop living at home like a recluse; get out into [go and face] the world (again); become a social being (again).

美脚【びきゃく】 beautiful [sexy, luscious] legs.
✧美脚効果 the effect of making *one's* legs look beautiful.
✧美脚効果抜群のジーパン jeans that make the legs look gorgeous.
✧美脚パンツ sexy pants; pants that show off ...'s legs (to the full).

引く【ひく】 ★⇨どんびき
✧突然愛を告白されて引いてしまった．I recoiled when he blurted out that he loved me.
✧ドラマは主人公が魅力的でないと引いちゃうよなあ．It turns me off if the hero of a show is unattractive.
✧彼が必死に演技すればするほど観客は引くばかりだった．The more effort he put into his act, the less interested [more apathetic] the audience was.

美形【びけい】 ⇨ビジュアルけい

日サロ【ひサロ】 ⇨ひやけサロン

ビシバシ, ビシビシ 〔厳しく〕 severely; rigorously; strictly; 〔激しく〕unrelentingly; relentlessly; ruthlessly; 〔精力的に〕energetically; vigorously.

◇ビシバシ鍛える[仕込む] discipline [train] strictly.
◇(…を)ビシバシ取り締まる enforce strict discipline; exercise rigid control (over ...).
◇ビシバシ叱る scold severely.
◇ビシバシひっぱたく thrash [spank] hard [soundly].
◇仕事をビシバシこなす put a lot of energy into *one's* work [job].

ビジュアル系【ビジュアルけい】, 美形【びけい】〔美貌〕good looks; comeliness; 〔美女〕a beautiful woman; 〔美男〕a good-looking man. ★⇨イケメン

◇美形の〔美貌の〕beautiful; comely; good-looking.
◇ビジュアル系の(バンド) garish; "visual-type" (rock band).

美少女【びしょうじょ】 a lovely [pretty, beautiful] young girl; a pretty [cute] little girl.

◇美少女アニメ an animated cartoon featuring pretty young girls.
◇美少女キャラ a pretty girl cartoon character. ★日本語の「美少女・美少年」を縮めた bishies (美形キャラ) という隠語もある. ⇨アニメ
◇美少女ゲーム a simulation (video) game featuring pretty young girls. ★⇨ギャルゲー
◇美少女コミック an adult comic featuring pretty young girls.
◇美少女フィギュア a three-dimensional figure of a pretty girl cartoon character. ★⇨フィギュア

美尻パンツ【びじりパンツ】 hip huggers; trousers that end at the hips (not at the waist).

ピチピチギャル ⇨ギャル

ヒッキー ⇨ひきこもり

ピッキング〔錠前破り〕(lock) picking. ★⇨サムターンまわし
◇ピッキングする pick a lock.
◇ピッキングに強い錠 a pick-free [pick-resistant] lock
◇近ごろピッキングによる空き巣被害が多発している. Recently, lock pickers [lock-picking burglars] have broken into many houses whose occupants were away.

ビックラこく
◇ビックラこいた！ Mercy!; 〔口語〕Well I'll be damned!; Strike a light!; I was flabbergasted [dum(b)founded].

びっくり水【びっくりみず】(a small amount of) cold water added to a boiling pot.
◇びっくり水を入れる add a little cold water (to prevent boiling over).

必勝【ひっしょう】
◇必勝だるま a victory *daruma* (doll).
◇必勝鉢巻き a victory headband.

ひっつき虫【ひっつきむし】〔動物や人間に付着するとげのある種〕a burr.

一人ご飯【ひとりごはん】eating alone (as opposed to eating with *one's* family).

ビニ本【ビニぼん】a skin magazine sold sealed in plastic film.

美乳【びにゅう】beautiful [lovely] breasts.

美白【びはく】beautiful white skin; whitening.
◇美白する whiten the skin; make the skin whiter.
◇美白化粧品 skin-whitening cosmetics; a skin whitener.
◇美白効果 a skin-whitening effect.
◇美白成分〔化粧品の〕a skin-whitening agent.

美肌【びはだ】beautiful [fair] skin;〔美容〕skin care.
◇美肌効果 skin enhancement.

ビビる get scared [frightened, nervous]; get a fright;〔…を見て〕shrink at [from] ...; quail at ...;〔口語〕get cold feet; go into a funk; get [have] the jitters; have [get] butterflies in *one's* stomach.
◇高速道路でスリップしたときはちょっとびびった．I got rather a fright when I skidded on the expressway.

ビミョー，微妙〔あいまいな返事〕hum; hmmm; well; Well, I'm not sure.;〔口語〕Beats me.;〔肯定しにくい時〕Well, I don't know about that.
◇「うまく行くのか？」「うーん，ビミョーっすね」"Will it work?" "Well, I don't know [I'm not sure].”

姫系【ひめけい】
◇フリフリの(＝フリルなどのひらひらした装飾が多い)姫系ファッション the frilly little-princess fashion look.

ヒモ〔情夫〕a pimp; a gigolo;〔食材としての貝の外套膜〕a

mantle.
◇女の**ヒモ**をやって暮らす live on the earnings of a woman; be a pimp.
◇アカガイの**ひも** an ark shell [*akagai*] filament [fringe].

非モテ【ひモテ】〔もてない〕be not welcomed; be unwelcome; be given a cold shoulder;〔人気がない〕be unpopular.
◇**非モテ**男 a man unpopular with women;〔ブサイクな〕an ugly [unattractive] man. ★⇨モテお

日焼けサロン【ひやけサロン】a tanning parlor [salon].

百均【ひゃっきん】，百円ショップ【ひゃくえんショップ】a 100-yen store [shop]. ★「百円均一で売る」は "sell at a uniform price of ¥100", 掲示の「このコーナー百円均一」は "Anything on this table (costs) ¥100." のように言える．

ヒュードロドロ
◇〔幽霊の出る場面で〕**ヒュードロドロ**の音とともに舞台は暗転した．An eerie wailing sound accompanied by a drumroll was heard as the stage went dark.

ヒューヒュー！
〔のろけ話を聞いて〕Yes, yes! We know she's [he's] wonderful.;〔熱い仲を見せつけられて「続きは二人きりのときにしてくれ」の意で〕That'll do! Wait till later [you're at home].;〔俗語〕Get a room! ★街頭でいい女に向かって「ヒュー」と口笛を鳴らすことを英語では wolf whistle と言う．

氷河期【ひょうがき】
〔就職難の〕a very serious situation [an "ice age"] for job hunters; an extremely tight labor market.
◇超氷河期 a desperate situation for job hunters; a situation in which there are simply no jobs at all.
◇今は…にとって就職氷河期だ．The job situation for . . . is desperate.

秒殺(する)【びょうさつ(する)】
trounce; give . . . a drubbing; beat [dispose of] . . . easily.
◇彼は挑戦者を秒殺で沈めた．He gave the challenger a drubbing without even having to try hard.
◇あんなやつは秒殺で片付けてやる．I can beat a guy like that hands down [without even trying].

ピラティス
〔商標〕Pilates (Method) ★ドイツ出身の考案者の名前から．発音は「ピラーティズ」に近い．

ヒラリーマン，平(社員)【ひら(しゃいん)】
a rank-and-file salaryman [salary woman]; a rank-and-file [lowly] employee; (just) an ordinary employee; a rank-and-file employee; nobody special in the company.
◇平社員のくせに課長の私に逆らおうというのかね．What's a nobody like you doing disobeying me like that? I'm the section chief!
◇平社員を大事にしない会社は発展しない．Companies that don't

look after their ordinary employees [the rank and file] don't grow.

ピン 〔一人で芸などをすること;「ピン」は「ピンからキリまで」と同じく「1」の意から〕

✧彼はコンビを組んでいるが**ピン**で活動することが多い．He's part of a group but often appears on stage or TV alone.
✧**ピン**芸人 a stand-up comedian. ★客の前で立ったまま漫談をする芸人の意．英米のコメディアンはこちらの方が多い．

ピン札【ピンさつ】 a brand-new [crisp] banknote.

✧手の切れるような**ピン札** a banknote so new that you could cut your hand on it.

ビン底メガネ，瓶底眼鏡【びんぞこめがね】

coke-bottle [milk-bottle] glasses; bottle bottom glasses; nerd glasses ★「nerd（ガリ勉，おたく）がかけるようなメガネ」の意；pebble glasses.

貧乳【ひんにゅう】small [tiny] breasts; a flat chest.
◇**貧乳女** a flat-chested woman. ★⇨せんたくいた，むね

ピンピンコロリ〔ピンピンと元気に長生きして安らかにコロリと死ぬこと〕staying hale and hearty (into old age) and then just popping off painlessly.
◇私も祖父のように**ピンピンコロリ**という具合に行きたいものだ．I hope I'll stay in good shape into old age and then when the time comes just pop off like that [keel over and die], like my grandfather.

ピンポ(ー)ン〔チャイムの音〕ding-dong. ★⇨ブー
◇**ピンポン**と玄関のベルが鳴った．The doorbell went ding-dong.
◇正解すると**ピンポン**，はずれるとブーッという音がします．Correct answers are signaled with a chime, incorrect ones with a buzzer.
◇**ピンポーン**！（＝正解，当たり！）That's it!; You're [That's] right!; Spot on!
◇**ピンポンダッシュ**〔玄関ベルを押して逃げるいたずら〕ringing a doorbell and running away; a runaway ring (of a doorbell); ding dong ditch.

ヒヤリハット〔あわや事故になりかかってヒヤリとしたりハッとしたりした経験〕a small incident [a near-miss] that gives one a shock; getting a fright about a potentially dangerous mistake; a scary minor incident; a close call.
◇**ヒヤリハット**体験 an experience of a scary [chilling, potentially dangerous] incident; a near-miss experience; a close call.

ヒヤリハット

✧ヒヤリハット報告 a report on a potentially dangerous minor incident; an incident report.

ふ

ファザコン〔ファーザー・コンプレックス〕a woman's [girl's] strong attachment for [to] her father; an Electra complex. ★⇨マザコン

フィギュア an action figure. ★⇨びしょうじょ，ソフビにんぎょう

Vシネ(マ)【ブイシネ(マ)】〔ビデオリリース用のB級映画〕a direct-to-video [straight-to-video] movie [film, release]; a film shot for video release.

ブイブイ言わせる【ブイブイいわせる】〔景気よくやる〕gain [have] a reputation as a big spender.

プー〔定職のない人，風太郎〕an idle person with no regular job;〔住所不定の人〕a vagabond; a person of no fixed abode [address].

ブー(ッ)〔クラクションの音〕beep; honk;〔ブザーの音〕buzz. ★⇨ブーイング，ピンポン
◇アタシが結婚する？ ブーッ．結婚するのは姉さんよ．Me? Getting married? Bosh! It's my sister that's getting married.
◇(…が不満で)ブーブー言う grumble (at [over, about]...); mutter (about...); complain (of...); gripe (at [about]...);〔口語〕beef (about...).

ブーイング〔やじること〕booing;〔やじの声〕(a) boo.
◇観客のブーイングで中断される be interrupted by the audience's

boos
✧ブーイングで役者を舞台から引っ込ませる boo an actor off the stage.
✧観客からブーイングの声が上がった．A few boos came from the audience.

風俗【ふうぞく】〔性産業〕the sex trade [business]; entertainment with a sexual implication.
✧風俗で働く work in the sex trade.
✧近くに風俗の店ができた．A sex-related business has opened nearby.
✧風俗営業を取り締まる regulate sex-related businesses; adult entertainment businesses.
✧風俗(関連)産業 the sex(-related) industry.
✧風俗嬢 a woman who works in the sex trade;〔ヘルス嬢〕a masseuse.
✧風俗店 a sex establishment;〔売春させる店〕a brothel; a massage parlor (offering sexual services).

プータロー，風太郎，プー太郎 ⇨プー

風評被害【ふうひょうひがい】damage caused by rumors.

ブーブー ⇨ブー

フェチ〔偏愛・執着〕a fetish; obsession.
✧靴フェチだ have a fetish for shoes.
✧胸フェチの男 titman, breastman.
✧脚フェチ legman.
✧尻フェチ ass man.

フェラ(チオ)　fellatio;〔卑語〕(a) blow job.
◇フェラをする fellate; perform fellatio on ...;〔卑語〕give head.

フォーク並び【フォークならび】
◇ATMでフォーク並びする wait in a single line until an ATM becomes available.

覆面【ふくめん】
◇**覆面**作家 an anonymous author.
◇**覆面**捜査官[員] an undercover police officer; a police officer working undercover;〔口語〕an undercover cop; an undercover (FBI) agent.
◇**覆面**パトカー an unmarked patrol car.

老け顔【ふけがお】
◇老け顔だ look older than *one's* age; look old for *one's* age.

不幸の手紙【ふこうのてがみ】chain mail [a chain letter] that promises you bad luck if you break the chain.

不思議ちゃん【ふしぎちゃん】〔何を考えているのかわからない，一風変わった少女〕an eccentric [a strange, a spacey] girl; Little Miss Spacey.　★⇨てんねん

豚箱【ブタばこ】a jail cell; a lockup;〔俗語〕the slammer.
◇ブタ箱にぶち込まれる be detained in a jail cell; be thrown in the slammer.

ふたまた，二股　★⇨うわき
◇彼女は鈴木君と田中君にふたまたかけているどころか，もっと彼氏がいる．Far from taking up with just Suzuki and Tanaka,

she has other boyfriends besides.

プチ… 〔小さい〕 petit(e); mini-; small.
◇プチ家出 running away (from home) for a short time.
◇プチ整形 minor cosmetic [plastic] surgery; a minor cosmetic (surgical) procedure.
◇プチ断食 a mini fast; a mini-fast.
◇プチボラ(＝ささやかなボランティア)する do a little (bit of) volunteer work.
◇プチ切れする 〔少しむかっとする[切れる]こと〕 throw a little fit; have a little (temper) tantrum. ★⇨ブチぎれる

ブチ切れる 【ブチぎれる】，ブチッと切れる 【ブチッときれる】 〔口語〕 blow up; blow *one's* top; explode; see red; 〔俗語〕 lose it. ★⇨キレる，プッツンする，プチ

プチプチ 〔小さな気泡状の突起が並んだ梱包材〕 bubble wrap.
◇プチプチをつぶして遊ぶ have fun [enjoy *oneself*] popping bubble wrap.

ぶっちぎり breaking away from the field; a breakaway; getting [pulling] far ahead of the field; opening up a wide gap between *oneself* and the field [the nearest runner].
◇ぶっちぎりの優勝 winning [a win, a victory] by a huge margin. ★⇨だんトツ

ぶっちゃける confess; come clean; own up (to) . . . ; tell frankly.
◇ぶっちゃけ(た話) 〔正直に言うと〕 to tell you the truth . . . ; let me give it to you straight . . . ; . . . to be frank . . . ; to put things

bluntly . . . .

プッツンする 〔自制できなくなる〕lose control of *oneself*; 〔かっとなる〕lose *one's* temper; 〔気がふれる〕go insane. ★⇨ブチぎれる，こわれる

フットバス 〔足浴器〕a footbath; a foot spa.

筆下ろし【ふでおろし】〔男の初体験〕a man's first sexual experience; losing *one's* virginity. ★⇨チェリーボーイ
◇**筆下ろし**をする have *one's* first sexual experience; lose *one's* virginity.

武闘派【ぶとうは】
◇**武闘派**ヤクザ a gang of vicious thugs.
◇彼女はおとなしそうに見えるが社内きっての**武闘派**だ．She looks as meek as a lamb, but at work she's tougher than anyone.

プニプニ，プヨプヨ
◇**プニプニ**[**プヨプヨ**]した springy; bouncy.
◇赤ちゃんの肌は**プニプニ**で気持ちがいい．I like the way a baby's skin is soft but resilient.
◇グミの**プニプニ**の食感が好きだ．I like the rubbery texture of gummi candy.

冬太り【ふゆぶとり】winter's waist. ★⇨くっちゃね，しょうがつぶとり
◇**冬太り**する put on weight in the winter.

ぶら下がり取材【ぶらさがりしゅざい】an on-the-move interview（with . . .）.

ブラハラ〔「ブラッドタイプ(血液型)」+「ハラスメント」;血液型で人の扱いを差別すること〕discriminating against people on the basis of their blood group. ★⇨セクハラ, パワハラ

ぶらり旅【ぶらりたび】
◇ぶらり旅に出る set out on a trip with no particular destination in mind; go on a journey without any particular destination in mind.

フリーター〔フリー・アルバイター〕a "freeter"; a permanent part-timer; a person who intentionally works part-time.

プリクラ a photo sticker;〔プリクラを撮る装置, プリ機〕a photo sticker machine; "Print Club."

振り込め詐欺【ふりこめさぎ】〔電話や手紙でだましたり恐喝したりして現金を銀行口座に振り込ませようとする詐欺;オレオレ詐欺(★⇨おれ)など〕a fraud in which the victim is deceived [threatened] into remitting money to a bank account; a remittance scam.

プリ帳【プリちょう】〔プリクラを貼る手帳〕an album for mounting *purikura* photo prints.

プリ帳のページの一例

ブリっ子【ブリッコ】
a girl who consciously cultivates an image of sweetness or tweeness; a girl who is cutesy; a cutesy girl; a "cutie girl."

フリフリ
⇨ひめけい

プリプリ
⇨プリンプリン

フリマ
〔蚤(のみ)の市，フリーマーケット〕a flea market.
★free market は経済用語の「(関税などの制限の無い)自由市場」の意.
◇フリマボックス〔レンタルスペースで収集品や手作り作品を並べて売る展示ケースの商標〕a rental display box.

プリンプリン，プリプリ
〔弾力がある様子〕plump; bouncy.
◇プリプリした歯ごたえ[食感]の tender and chewy
◇プリプリのエビ(の入った餃子) (pot stickers filled with) chewy shrimp
◇プリプリしたほっぺた plump [chubby] cheeks.
◇プリプリの煮こごりが出来た．The broth has jelled nice and bouncy.
◇プリンプリンと揺れるあのヒップがたまらない．I just love the way her bottom jiggles.

ブルー
◇ブルーになる be [feel, get] depressed; feel [be] down [low]; sink into [be in] low spirits. ★⇨へこむ
◇今日はちょっとブルーな気分．I'm feeling a bit down [low] today.
◇ブルーなときに聞くといい曲だよ．It's a nice piece to listen to

when your spirits are low.
◆ちょっとブルー入ってるときに優しい言葉をかけられてほろりとした. When I was feeling blue, his kind words really touched me.

ブルセラ 〔女子中高生が着用していたブルマー・セーラー服・下着類〕 used underwear and uniforms of schoolgirls.
◆ブルセラショップ a "burusera" shop; a shop that sells underwear and uniforms of schoolgirls.

フルチン male frontal nudity; letting it all hang out.

ブレーク[ブレイク]する burst onto the scene.
◆来年ブレークすると予想される芸能人 an entertainer [actor, actress] who is expected to become popular [have a big break] next year.
◆大ブレークしたのは 2002 年のことだった. The big break came in 2002.

ブログ a Web log; a blog. ★⇨えんじょう

プロフ 〔ネット・携帯の自己紹介(プロフィール)サイト〕 a profile site.

分煙【ぶんえん】 separation of smoking and nonsmoking areas; 〔職場の〕 division of a workplace into smoking and nonsmoking areas.
◆完全分煙 complete [total] separation of smoking and nonsmoking areas.
◆不完全分煙 semi-separation [incomplete separation] of smoking and nonsmoking areas.

◆この店は不完全**分煙**だ．The place doesn't separate smoking and nonsmoking areas completely [thoroughly, properly].
◆公共空間の**分煙**化を推進する promote the division [separation] of public spaces into smoking and nonsmoking areas.

へ

ペア
◇ペア鑑賞券[チケット，入場券] a two-person theater [concert] ticket.
◇ペアシート〔電車・レストランなどの〕a two-person seat; a double seat;〔映画館などの〕a love seat.
◇ペアルック the pair look; the appearance of two people wearing identical clothes.
◇ペアルックの2人 two people [a couple] wearing identical clothes.
◇太郎と花子は堂々とペアルックで登校した．Taro and Hanako weren't afraid to turn up at school in matching clothes.

ぺえぺえ，ペーペー
◇ペーペーの inferior; low-class; lowly; petty; minor; humble; poor.
◇ペーペーの新米看護師 an (ignorant) inexperienced nurse.
◇私のようなペーペーは看板スターたちの使いっ走りもしなければならない．A lowly being like me has to go running around [round] on errands for famous stars.
◇ペーペー役者 a poor actor; a utility man; the utility.

へこむ 〔…にやりこめられる〕be beaten; be squelched; (be forced to) yield [give in] to ...;〔しょげる〕become disheartened [demoralized]; become downcast.
◇あの人は何を言われてもへこまない．He won't let himself be beaten by anything.; Nothing will daunt him.
◇思い切って髪型を変えたら，みんなに前のほうがよかったと

言われてへこんだ．After I took the plunge and changed my hairstyle, everyone said they preferred it as it was before, which really got me down.

へそ
✧へそピアス navel [belly button] piercing.
✧へそピアスをする have one's navel pierced (for a ring); have a ring [stud] in one's navel; have a belly ring.
✧へそ出しルック a (bare-)midriff look.

ベタ
✧ベタな筋立て hackneyed [trite, quite predictable] plot.

ヘタこく ⇨こく

ヘタウマ 〔一見下手のようだが実は巧みなこと〕good badness; skilled unskillfulness.
✧へたうまのイラスト a simple but well-done line drawing.

ヘタレ worthlessness; laziness; weakness; incompetence; wimpiness. ★⇨だめ
✧ヘタレな worthless; lazy; weak; incompetent; wimpy.
✧ヘタレ技術者 a poor excuse for an engineer.

◇**ヘタレ**監督 an incompetent director.
◇**ヘタレ**っぷり a show [display] of *one's* worthlessness.
◇**ヘタレ**な私の**ヘタレ**な一日を書いた日記 a diary entry describing a do-nothing day spent by do-nothing me.
◇この**ヘタレ**な性格，大学入っても直りません．My loser personality won't change even if I do get into college.
◇あんな**ヘタレ**にこの仕事ができるもんか．There's no way such a useless [hopeless, pathetic] guy could do this job.; You can't expect an idiot like him to do this work.

ペチャパイ　⇨ひんにゅう

別居【べっきょ】 separation;〔夫婦の〕limited divorce;〔法律上の〕legal [judicial] separation.
◇(…と)**別居**する live in a separate house; live separately; live apart (from ...); set up separate residences; separate.
◇**別居**中の夫[妻] a separated husband [wife]．★⇨かよいづま
◇**別居**(結)婚〔仕事で離れて暮らすが週末などに一緒になる〕a commuter marriage.
◇家庭内**別居**⇨かていない
◇**別居**はどれくらい続いたのか？ How long had they been separated?
◇**別居**はしたが，離婚はしなかったらしい．There had been a separation, but apparently no divorce.

別腹【べつばら】
◇おなかいっぱいだけど，ケーキは**別腹**よ．I'm full, but I could fit in [there should be room for] some cake.

ヘボい　⇨ヘタレ，だめ

ヘルス ⇨ふうぞく

変顔【ヘンがお】
◆〔カメラなどに向かって〕**変顔**をして見せる make a (funny) face.

変身ロボ【へんしんロボ】 ⇨がったいロボ

ヘンタイ，変態 〔変質者・異常者〕a degenerate; a pervert; a deviate; a deviant;〔口語〕a perv; a sicko.
◆そんなことを言ってると**ヘンタイ**扱いされるぞ．Talk about that sort of thing, and people around you will be bound to treat you as abnormal [a pervert].

ペン回し【ペンまわし】〔指先でボールペンやシャーペンなどを回す遊び〕pen spinning.

ほ

ポイ捨て【ポイすて】littering.
　◇ポイ捨てする throw away.
　◇ポイ捨て禁止条例 an ordinance against littering.

ボイスパーカッション，ボイパ〔口で打楽器の音をまねる技術〕vocal percussion.

ボイン　⇨きょにゅう，むね

放送禁止用語【ほうそうきんしようご】words whose use is prohibited on radio and television;〔タブーとなっている語〕taboo [tabooed] word;〔一般的に下品・卑猥とされる禁句〕four letter word ★英語では shit（クソ），cunt（女のあそこ），fuck（やる），piss（ションベン）など4文字が多いことから．⇨ピー

暴走族【ぼうそうぞく】〔1人〕a member of a motorcycle [car] gang;〔集団〕a motorcycle [car] gang;〔口語〕bikers; hot-rodders. ★⇨レディース

ほおかぶり ⇨ほっかぶり

ボカスカ ⇨ボコボコ

ぼく的【ぼくてき】 ⇨わたしてき

ボケ 〔漫才の〕the funnyman. ★⇨つっこみ
♦ボケとツッコミ the fool and the straight man (of a pair of stand-up comedians); the dumb and the witty roles that draw laughter from the audience in *manzai*.
♦ボケをかます slip up; make [let slip] a boo-boo.
♦この大ボケ野郎. You really are a stupid idiot.
♦天然ボケ ⇨てんねん.
♦ぼけ倒す ⇨…たおす

保健室登校【ほけんしつとうこう】 (going to school but) just staying [spending the whole day] in the sickroom.

ホコ天【ホコてん】〔歩行者天国〕a "pedestrians' paradise" (temporarily closed to motor traffic); a pedestrian mall [precinct]; a (weekend) traffic-free zone.

ボコボコにする, ボコる beat ... up; beat up on ...; beat ... to (a) pulp; give ... a thorough thrashing; beat ...'s brains out; wipe the floor with ...; give ... the works.
♦ボコボコにされる get knocked around in a fight; be given a good thumping.
♦あいつをボコボコにしてやった. I beat the living daylights out of him.; I beat [thrashed] him to within an inch of his life.

ポシャる flop; fizzle out; go phut; be wrecked.

ホタル族【ホタルぞく】
the firefly people (the glow of whose cigarettes pulse in the dark), who have to smoke outside their house or on the veranda of their flat because other family members dislike cigarette smoke.

ボチボチ
◇「どうです景気は？」「まあ，**ボチボチ**ですわ」"How's business?" "Just so so.; I'm managing.; I keep my head above water (but only just)."

ほっかぶり，ほおかぶり
◇ほっかぶりする〔布で〕wrap a cloth over *one's* head and cheeks and tie it under *one's* chin;〔知らん顔する〕pretend not to notice [know about] ...; bury *one's* head in the sand.

ぼったくる，ぼる
(intentionally) overcharge; make undue [indecent] profits; profiteer; charge ... an exorbitant price (for ...);〔口語〕soak;〔俗語〕rip off .
◇ぼったくりバー〔俗語〕a rip-off bar; a clip joint.
◇ぼったくり防止条例 an ordinance against charging exorbitant prices.

◇客からぼ(ったく)る店 a shop that overcharges [charges exorbitantly, rips customers off].
◇どうもタクシーにぼったくられたらしい．I have a feeling I was ripped off by that taxi driver.

ぼっちゃん【坊ちゃん】⇨おぼっちゃん

ぽっと出【ぽっとで】
◇ぽっと出のタレント a new entertainer fresh to the scene.

ポテチ〔ポテトチップス〕potato chips ★英国では普通 potato crisps.

ホの字【ホのじ】
◇あいつあの子にホの字だ．He's crazy [gaga] about her.
◇あんたあの子にホの字だね．You have a thing about [crush on] her, don't you?

誉め殺し【ほめごろし】mockery [ridicule] by overpraising; damning with lavish praise; a backhanded compliment.
◇誉め殺しにする praise sb with the intention of mocking him [her]．★⇨…たおす(誉め倒す)

ぼる ⇨ぼったくる

ボン・キュッ・ボン〔胸とヒップがボンと出てウエストがキュッと引き締まったセクシーな体型〕★⇨ナイスバディ
◇彼女はボン・キュッ・ボンで抜群のプロポーションだ．She has fine proportions and an hourglass figure.; She is voluptuous and wasp-waisted. ★英米ではスリーサイズをインチ(約 2.5 セ

ンチ)で表わして She is a perfect 36-24-36. (上から 90, 60, 90 (センチ) の完璧なプロポーションだ) のように言うことも多い.

本ちゃん【ほんちゃん】, 本番【ほんばん】
〔舞台などの〕acting for [before] an audience;〔映画の〕acting for filming [before the camera]; a take;〔ラジオ・テレビの〕going on the air.

◇**本番**でせりふを忘れてしまった. I forgot my lines on stage [on air].

◇〔映画の撮影で〕**本番**です. お静かに願います. Quiet, please. This will be a take.

◇〔ポルノ映画で〕**本番**(＝実際の性交)をやる perform unsimulated [actual] sex.

本命【ほんめい】
◇**本命**の大学 *one's* first-choice university.

◇**本命**チョコ〔バレンタインデーの〕a heartfelt (rather than obligatory) gift of chocolate to a man on Valentine's Day. ★⇨ ぎりチョコ, ともチョコ

ま

マイ… 〔自分専用の〕one's own; personal; for one's own use.
◇マイシューズ[ボール]〔ボウリング用の〕one's own [personal] bowling shoes [balls].
◇マイ箸 one's own [personal] chopsticks (for use when dining out).
◇マイバッグ〔レジ袋の代わりに，自宅から持参する買い物袋〕one's own shopping [carrier] bag.
◇マイブーム〔個人的に入れ込んでいること〕a personal (temporary) mania.

前説【まえせつ】〔本番前の〕a warm-up performance.

真逆【まぎゃく】
◇真逆な[の] exactly the opposite; just the opposite.
◇〔本当は好きなのに〕いざ彼女に会うと本心と真逆のことを言ってしまう．When it actually comes to meeting her I always say just the opposite of [something completely different from] what I really think.

枕営業【まくらえいぎょう】〔肉体関係を利用して仕事を取る営業〕providing sexual favors to promote one's business [career];〔口語〕sleeping one's way to success;〔芸能界でいい役をもらうための〕the casting couch.

…まくる 〔さかんに…する〕do ... all around; do a great deal of .... ★⇨…たおす
◇しゃべりまくる talk and talk; talk [jabber, chat] on and on.

◆あちこちに電話をかけ**まくる** phone all around [over the place]; call everywhere [everyone] (one can think of).

負け組【まけぐみ】 the losing [defeated] side [team, group]; the losers.

マザコン 〔マザーコンプレックス〕 a mother complex [fixation]; an Oedipus complex; a man's [boy's] strong attachment for [to] his mother;〔マザコンの男〕a mother's [mama's] boy.

マジ
◆マジかよ． You can't be serious.; You can't mean it.
◆彼女，マジで生徒会長に立候補するつもりらしい． It seems she really is going to run for the student council chair.
◆あいつ，お前にマジで惚れてるぜ． She's crazy [head over heels] about you.;〔俗語〕She's got a major crush on you.
◆えっ！ マジ(で)？ What! Really?; Seriously?; Do you mean that?; Straight up?
◆マジ切れする (completely) lose control (of *one's* temper);〔俗語〕get really pissed off; (totally) lose it.

マスオさん 〔漫画『サザエさん』でサザエの夫であるフグ田マスオから，妻の実家に同居している男性〕a husband who lives with his wife in a house that belongs to her parents.

マスト・アイテム 〔必需品〕a must item; a must-have (item).

まずる 〔どじを踏む〕blunder;〔口語〕goof up;〔俗語〕blow it.
◆まずったなあ． Now I've (really) blown it!

待受け（画面）【まちうけ（がめん）】〔携帯電話の〕a standby (display) screen; (a) cellphone [mobile phone] wallpaper.

街金（融），町金（融）【まちきん（ゆう）】〔高利貸し〕a loan shark (company);〔高利金融業〕loan sharking. ★⇨サラきん, やみ（闇金）

まったり
◇まったりした甘み a rich sweetness.
◇まったりした口当たり a full-bodied flavor.
◇まったりとした生活 a laid-back [relaxed, comfortable] lifestyle;the life of Riley.
◇まったりする feel easy [at ease]; relax; take it easy; feel [make *oneself*] at home.
◇温泉にでも行ってまったりしたいなあ．It sure would be nice to go (off) to a hot spring and relax for a while.

マッチョ a macho (man). ★⇨ムキムキ

マッパ〔真っ裸〕with nothing on; stark-naked; in the nude; in *one's* bare skin;〔口語〕in the altogether;〔口語〕(all) in the buff. ★ buff は元来「牛などの革」を指し，転じて「人の素肌, 素っ裸」の意．⇨フルチン
◇…をマッパにする strip ... of all ...'s clothes; strip ... (down) naked.
◇マッパにされる be stripped of *one's* clothes [to the skin,〔口語〕to the buff].

マナーモード〔携帯電話の〕the silent mode; the silent ring [silent-ring] mode.
◇ケータイをマナーモードにする put *one's* (cellular) phone into

silent mode.

マブダチ 〔口語〕a tight friend. ★⇨ダチ

ママチャリ 〔買い物用自転車〕a bike used for shopping. ★⇨チャリ

ママドル 〔子供のいる女性アイドルタレント〕female TV personality who is both a mother and a former teenage media star.

マヨラー 〔どんな料理にもマヨネーズをかけて食べる人〕a mayonnaise addict; somebody who puts mayonnaise on everything he [she] eats.

マルガリーマン 〔丸刈りのサラリーマン〕a salaryman who shaves his head (in imitation of fashionable sportsmen).

マル査【マルサ】〔国税査察官の俗称〕a national tax inspector; 〔俗語〕a tax dick.

丸文字【まるもじ】rounded handwriting. ★⇨ギャル（ギャル文字）

マン喫，漫喫【マンきつ】〔漫画喫茶〕a coffee shop with a *manga* library. ★⇨ネット（ネットカフェ）

み

ミーハー
◇近くでドラマのロケがあると聞いて飛んでいくなんて，君もミーハーだねえ．Running over to see when you hear they're filming a drama nearby! You're something of the follow-the-crowd type, aren't you?
◇髪型や服装に着目するようなミーハー層がその政治家の人気を支えている．That politician is supported by tagalongs who are attracted to her hairstyle and clothes.
◇また私設応援団やるのか，お前もミーハーだな．Starting another of your fan clubs are you? What a faddist you are!
◇ミーハー女[男] a trendy woman [man].

見え見え【みえみえ】 ⇨バレバレ

みかじめ料【みかじめりょう】〔やくざが店から取り立てる用心棒代〕protection money.

右肩上がり【みぎかたあがり】
◇右肩上がりで増加する increase steadily.

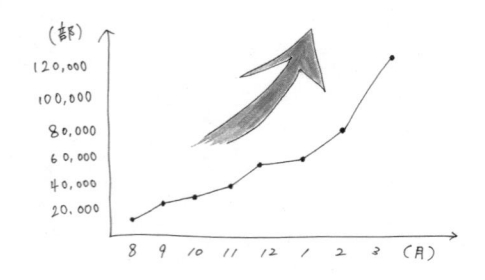

✧**右肩上がり**の経済成長 a continuously [steadily] growing economy.
✧**右肩上がり**の時代は終わった．The days of a continuously growing economy are over [are history].

ミスコン　a beauty contest.

ミスる
✧あ，**ミスっ**た！　Oops!; Oh no!; Damn !

見せパン【みせパン】〔ローライズからのぞかせるパンティ〕show-off panties; fancy panties.

見せブラ【みせブラ】〔肩ひもをのぞかせるブラジャー〕a show-off bra; a fashion bra.

耳がダンボ【みみがダンボ】
✧**耳がダンボ**になる〔全身が耳になる（ほど熱心に聞く）〕be all ears;〔聞き耳を立てる〕prick up *one's* ears.

耳タコ【みみタコ】〔耳にタコができるほど〕
✧…はもう聞き飽きて**耳タコ**だ get sick of hearing ...
✧その話はもう**耳タコ**だよ．I've heard that so often I've got calluses on my ears.

ミリめし　〔兵士が携行する戦闘糧食；military（軍隊の）と飯（めし）を組み合わせた造語〕military provisions; (military) rations.

む

ムカつく ★⇨キれる
◇〔怒って〕あームカつくー！ I'm fed up.; That makes me mad.
◇あいつ，ムカつくなあ．He makes me sick.; He's disgusting [irritating].
◇単に「ムカついたから」という理由で人に乱暴する子供が増えている．The number of children who attack a person just because they get angry at that person is increasing.
◇話を聞いているうちになんだかムカついてきた．While listening to that story I somehow got upset [felt worse and worse].

ムキムキ
◇彼は筋肉ムキムキの体が自慢だ．He's proud of his muscular [brawny] body.

ムズい 〔むずかしい〕hard; difficult.
◇第1問が激ムズかった．The first problem puzzled [beat] me.

息子 【むすこ】 ...'s thingy; ...'s whatsit; 〔卑語〕dick; cock.

無茶食い 【むちゃぐい】(just) eating and eating; gross overeating.

むちゃくちゃ, むっちゃ ⇨めちゃくちゃ

むっつりスケベ ★⇨スケベ
◇あいつはむっつりスケベだ．He's a lecher beneath his solemn veneer.

胸 【むね】 〔乳房〕 breasts. ★⇨きょにゅう, ひんにゅう, びにゅう

◇貧弱な胸 small [skinny, meager] breasts.

◇豊満な胸 well-developed [ample] breasts.

◇うちの娘も近ごろ胸がふっくらしてきた. Our daughter's breasts are beginning to develop lately.

◇彼女は胸がない[小さい]. She is flat-chested.; Her breasts are (so) small.

◇胸の谷間 a cleavage

◇胸の谷間を強調するブラジャー a cleavage-enhancing [push-up] bra. ★⇨よせる

◇胸の開いた服 low-cut clothes; clothes with a low neckline

◇胸の豊かな[大きい]女性 a full-bosomed [bosomy, busty] woman; a woman with well-developed breasts

◇胸の形がいい have beautiful breasts; have nicely-shaped breasts.

◇胸がキュンとなる, 胸キュンになる *one's* heart leaps.

◇愛し合う二人が別れるシーンで胸がキュンとなった. The scene where the two lovers part wrung my heart [really choked me up].

ムラムラ

◇彼はグラビアを見ているうちにムラムラしてきた. While looking at (the) gravure pictures, he became sexually aroused [excited].

むりくり 〔無理矢理に〕 by force; perforce; forcibly; by [with] a [the] strong arm [hand]; compulsorily; under compulsion; willy-nilly; pushily.

ムンムン

◇色気ムンムンの女[男] a very sexy woman [man].

め

メアド〔メールアドレスの略〕⇨メール

メイド喫茶[カフェ]【メイドきっさ[カフェ]】 a maid cafe.

メール〔電子メール〕an e-mail (message). ★日本語の「メール」と違い，英語では mail だけだと「郵便」が最も普通の意味だが，電子メールであることが文脈で明らかなら使える．また，仕組みは違うがメールと同じように携帯電話でやり取りできる文字通信（ショートメール）を text (message) または SMS〔short message service の略〕と呼び，「メールする」と同じような意味で text を動詞として使うことが多い．パソコンで「メールする」は send e-mail または mail を動詞として使う．⇨ケータイ
◇ファイルをメールで送る send a file via e-mail; mail a file.
◇メールにファイルを添付する attach a file to an e-mail message.
◇知らない人からのメールの添付ファイルを開かないように．Do not open e-mail attachments from unknown senders.
◇メールを開かなくてもウイルスに感染することがある．You can be infected with a virus without even opening the e-mail.
◇怪しいメールを削除する delete a suspicious e-mail
◇結論についてはメールを入れておきますので暇なときに見てください．I'll let you know the (final) decision by e-mail, so open it at your convenience.
◇毎朝出社したらメールをチェックする．Every morning when I am in the office, I check my e-mail.
◇メールアドレス，メ(ル)アド an e-mail address.
◇メール相手 *one's* e-mail correspondent(s). ★⇨メルとも

◇彼女とは毎日**メール**交換している．I exchange [trade] e-mail with her every day.
◇**メール**私語〔授業中に携帯でメールのやりとりをすること〕e-mailing secretly [sending secret e-mails] during class.
◇**メール**配信 e-mail distribution.
◇迷惑**メール** nuisance [junk, unwanted] (e-)mail; spam (mail).
◇迷惑**メール**対策ソフト anti-spam software; anti-junk mail software.

目が点になる 【めがてんになる】 look amazed [dazed, stunned].

メジャーデビュー 〔歌手の〕 *one's* major-label debut; 〔大リーグの〕 *one's* Major League debut; 〔ゴルフの〕 *one's* first (appearance in a) Major.
◇デモ CD がレコード会社に認められて昨年**メジャーデビュー**した．Their demo CD caught the fancy of a record company, and last year they made their major-label debut [released their first record through a major label].
◇桑田はパイレーツで念願の**メジャーデビュー**を果たした．Kuwata made his long-wished-for Major League debut with the Pirates.
◇国内**メジャーデビュー**戦で石川は苦戦した．Ishikawa struggled

in his first appearance in a domestic Major.

メタボ(リック)

✧メタボ腹〔太鼓腹〕a potbelly; a (prominent) paunch; a spare tire.

✧メタボ体形の男 a potbellied [paunchy] man.

✧メタボリックシンドローム〔代謝異常症候群〕metabolic syndrome.

目力【めぢから】〔目元の印象力〕eyes that convey a strong sense of purpose.

めちゃくちゃ, めっちゃ, めちゃめちゃ

✧めちゃくちゃ[むちゃくちゃ]な incoherent; absurd; unreasonable; preposterous.

✧めちゃくちゃな議論 a crazy argument.

✧めちゃくちゃなことを言う talk incoherently; talk nonsense; blabber (on).

✧こりゃめちゃくちゃだな．This is a terrible mess.; What an awful mess!

✧めっちゃタフな super tough.

✧うちの近くのコンビニ店員はめちゃくちゃかわいい．There's a girl working at the convenience store near my home who's totally cute.

◇成田空港でその女優を見かけたけど，**めちゃくちゃキレイだっ**たよ．I spotted that actress at Narita Airport—she's a real looker!
◇その俳優は近くで見ると**めちゃくちゃかっこよかった**．That actor's wicked cool close up.
◇**めちゃくちゃ高かった**よ．It was awfully expensive.; It cost a hell of a lot.
◇あの店のケーキ，**めちゃくちゃおいしい**よ．The cake at that shop is out of this world.
◇**めちゃくちゃでっかい** enormous; humongous.
◇金メダルが取れなくて**めっちゃ悔しい**．I could kill myself for not getting the gold.
◇**めちゃくちゃ勉強する** study like crazy; work like fury.
◇**めちゃくちゃほめる** go overboard in praising ...
◇**めちゃくちゃ楽しい**．That's great [wonderful]!; It's so much fun!
◇**めちゃくちゃ急いで** in wild haste.
◇**めちゃくちゃかわいがる** love blindly; dote on ...
◇あの映画は**めちゃくちゃおもしろかった**．That movie was simply great [wonderful, out of this world].

メディアジャック
〔広告スペースなどの一社独占〕single-sponsor advertising;〔電車内広告の〕advertising by only one company on a train.

メルアド
〔メールアドレスの略〕⇨メール

メル友【メルとも】
〔口語〕an e-pal; a key pal; a cyber friend [pal]; a cyberpal. ★⇨メール

メルヘンチック
◇**メルヘンチック**な物語 a fairy-tale-like story.

メロメロ

◇…にメロメロだ be far gone on . . . ; be head over heels in love with . . . ; be infatuated with . . . ; have a soft [weak] spot [place] (in *one's* heart) for . . .

メンチ切る【メンチきる】 ⇨ガンをつける

メンドい 〔面倒くさい〕

◇自分で行くなんてメンドいことするかよ. I don't bother to go there myself.

◇いちいち書き写すのはメンドいからコピーしよう. Copying them all out (by hand) is a pain (in the neck). Let's photocopy [xerox] them.; It's a drag having to copy each one separately. How about photocopying them?

◇もう歯を磨くのもメンドい. Even cleaning my teeth is a bother.

も

萌え 【もえ】〔…に感じる魅力〕a fascination with ...; an infatuation with ...; a crush on .... ★⇨なえ
◇萌えキャラ a cute [charming] character.
◇萌え要素 a cute [an attractive, a charming] feature [characteristic].
◇萌え系アニメキャラ "moe"-type anime characters. ★⇨アニメ

…モード〔…(な)状態〕(a) mode;〔…(な)気分〕a mood; a frame of mind; a mental [psychological] state;〔…の雰囲気・様子〕an impression; a mood; an atmosphere.
◇連日の残業ですっかりお疲れモードだよ．Working overtime day after day I'm in a state of exhaustion.
◇通訳をしているので，外国人へのインタビュー番組はつい仕事モードで見てしまう．Since I'm an interpreter, I can't help going into working mode when I see interviews with people from abroad on TV [I always find myself watching TV interviews with people from abroad in a professional frame of mind].
◇仕事モードになる go into working mode; get [put oneself] into a working frame of mind
◇休日出勤が続き，常に頭が仕事モードになっている．With repeated holiday shifts, I feel in working mode all the time.
◇連休が終わって今日から会社だ．仕事モードに切り替えなきゃ．Now the long weekend is over it's back to work at the company today. I must get back into working mode.
◇チームは初戦から本気モードで戦った．They played really seriously from the very first game.

モザイク 〔テレビなどで画像に入れるぼかし〕
   ◆テレビ映像に**モザイク**をかける obscure [blur, 〔口語〕mosaic] a TV image
   ◆**モザイク**画像 an obscured [a blurred, a mosaicked] TV image.
   ◆画面では容疑者の顔に**モザイク**がかけられていた．The suspect's face was obscured [covered, blurred out, mosaicked out] on the TV image.
   ◆被害者の顔に**モザイク**をかける obscure [blur, put mosaic over] a victim's face.
   ◆**モザイク**をはずす remove the blurring [mosaic].
   ◆**モザイク**をはずした画像 a deblurred image; an image with the blurring [mosaic] removed.

持ちネタ【もちネタ】 *one's* repertory (of tricks); acts that *one* can do. ★⇨ネタ
   ◆**持ちネタ**を披露する show people *one's* favorite party piece [parlor trick].

モチモチ，モッチリ 〔弾力のある〕puffy; springy.
   ◆**モチモチ**の肌 springy skin.
   ◆この麺は**モチモチ**した食感がある．These noodles have springy texture when you're eating them.
   ◆外はパリッとして，中は**モッチリ**感のあるパン bread crispy on the outside and spongy [soft] on the inside.

モテ男【モテお】a man very popular with women; a ladies' [lady's] man; a playboy; a beau; a gallant; a Romeo. ★⇨ひモテ, …キター
   ◆おまえけっこう**モテ男**じゃん．You've really got a way with the ladies, don't you?

モテモテ

◇(…に)**モテモテ**だ〔もてはやされる〕be made much of; be welcomed; be warmly [cordially] received; have a warm reception; be talked much of; be lionized;〔人気がある〕be popular with [among] . . . ; be in favor with . . . ; be a favorite with . . . .

◇きれいな女の子はいつも**モテモテ**だ．Pretty girls receive much attention.

◇彼はそのパーティーで**モテモテ**だった．He was having a great success at the party.

◇あいつは若い女性に**モテモテ**だ．He is very popular with [idolized by] young girls.

モデル立ち【モデルだち】 ⇨コンパニオンだち

元カノ【もとカノ】 a former girlfriend;〔口語〕*one's* ex. ★ex (エクス)は「前の」を意味する接頭辞を名詞化したもの．男女問わず，また別れた夫や妻にも使う．⇨いまカノ

元カレ【もとカレ】 a former boyfriend;〔口語〕*one's* ex. ★⇨いまカレ

元サヤ【もとサヤ】

◇**元サヤ**に納まる get back together.

◇前のダンナと**元サヤ**になる be reconciled with her former husband.

◇別れた亭主がわびを入れて結局二人は**元サヤ**にもどった．The pair were eventually reconciled after the woman's former husband made an apology.

元ネタ【もとネタ】 the source [inspiration] (for . . .); the origin (al) (of . . .).　★⇨ネタ

✧黒澤の映画『隠し砦の三悪人』に登場する農民コンビが『スター・ウォーズ』のロボットコンビの**元ネタ**であるのは有名な話だ． It is well known that the two farmers who appear in Kurosawa's movie "The Hidden Fortress" inspired the two robots in "Star Wars."

盛り下がる［下げる］【もりさがる［さげる］】

〔「盛り上がる［上げる］」の反対語〕 become dampened; be spoiled; turn sour. ★⇨ひく，ドンびき

✧楽しい場を**盛り下げて**しまう cast a chill over [spoil, put a damper on] a festive situation.

✧雰囲気を**盛り下げる**やつ a wet blanket; a kill-joy.

✧彼女が突然泣き出して完全に**盛り下がって**しまった． She suddenly broke (out) into tears, ruining the mood for everyone in the room.

✧そんな話は今するなよ．**盛り下がる**から． Don't talk about that now, okay? It spoils the mood.

モンスター・ペアレント

a parent who makes selfish and unreasonable demands on behalf of his child; a "monster parent."

や

八百長 【やおちょう】 fixing; rigging; a fix.
✧**八百長**で負ける〔勝ちをゆずる〕throw a match [game, race] to *one's* opponent.
✧**八百長**のけんか a put-up [staged] quarrel.
✧**八百長**をやる fix a fight; put in the fix.
✧**八百長**疑惑 (a) suspicion of match-fixing [game-fixing, race-fixing].
✧**八百長**競馬 a fixed [rigged] horse race.
✧**八百長**試合 a rigged [fixed] game; a put-up game.
✧**八百長**質問〔議員の〕a "fixed" interpellation. ★⇨やらせ
✧**八百長**質問をする put a planted [fixed] question; ask a put-up question.
✧**八百長**相撲 a rigged [fixed] sumo match; a fixed sumo bout.

焼き破り 【やきやぶり】〔窓ガラスを火であぶり音の出ないように割る盗みの手口〕breaking and entering by heating window glass so that it can be broken quietly.

野球拳 【やきゅうけん】 a game in which two people sing a short song and pantomime playing baseball followed by a round of rock-paper-scissors, with the loser removing one piece of clothing; strip baseball.

約一名 【やくいちめい】
✧まだ宿題を提出していない不届き者が**約一名**いるようだ. It appears that one irresponsible person who shall go unnamed has not yet submitted his homework.

ヤクザ 〔暴力団員〕a gangster; a yakuza;〔ならず者〕a good-for-nothing (fellow); a scamp; a rascal; a wastrel;〔ばくち打ち〕a gambler;〔ごろつき〕a hooligan; a hoodlum; a racketeer.
◇ヤクザの親分 an underworld boss
◇ヤクザの出入り a gang attack on a rival gang.
◇ヤクザ映画 a gangster movie; a yakuza movie.

やってられない，やってらんない
◇やってられないよ，まったく．I can't handle it anymore.; I'm completely fed up with it.
◇こんなに臭くて汚い仕事で月給15万じゃやってらんないよ．No way I can keep doing this dirty, smelly work for just 150,000 yen a month.

雇われ… 【やとわれ…】
◇雇われ店長 a hired store manager
◇雇われママ the hired head hostess of a drinking establishment.

ヤバい 〔危険な〕dangerous; risky; chancy; touch-and-go;〔違法な〕illegal;〔すごい，すてきな〕superb; wonderful; amazing; great; fantastic; terrific; awesome.
◇お前，かなりヤバいことになってるぞ．You're on very thin ice, my friend.
◇ヤベえ！ サツだ！ 逃げろ！ Uh-oh, the cops [Damn! It's the cops]. Let's get out of here.

闇… 【やみ…】 ★⇨うら…
◇闇金(融) illegal [black-market] loaning;〔口語〕loan-sharking.
◇闇金に手を出す get a loan through illegal channels.
◇闇サイト〔犯罪・自殺・中傷など反社会的目的のサイト〕an undesirable [objectionable, unsavory] site; a clandestine site.

やらせ
a staged [rehearsed, scripted] event; a put-on.
- ◇事故のやらせ staging [faking, feigning] an accident.
- ◇やらせっぽい give the impression of having been staged; seem [look] fake(d).
- ◇やらせの場面 a staged [faked] scene; a pseudoevent; a fabrication; a setup.
- ◇あの場面はやらせだった．That scene was staged [faked].
- ◇やらせ質問〔公聴会などでの〕a scripted [staged, planted, prearranged] question. ★⇨やおちょう

ヤンエグ
〔青年実業家；「ヤング」と「エグゼキュティヴ(重役・経営者)」(executive) をつなげた和製英語〕a young entrepreneur [manager]; an entrepreneurial [a managerial] kid.

ヤンキー
〔不良少年〕a (juvenile) delinquent; a (young) social rebel; an adolescent with an attitude. ★⇨ワル

ヤンキー座り 【ヤンキーずわり】
- ◇ヤンキー座りする squat with legs spread, heels pressed to the ground, and hands holding *one's* knees.

ヤンママ
〔昔ヤンキーだった若い母親〕a young mother who was a delinquent in her teens. ★⇨レディース

ゆ

UMA【ユーマ】〔「雪男」「ツチノコ」などの未確認動物〕a cryptid; an unsubstantiated species (of animal); a "mystery animal [species]." ★ UMA は unidentified mysterious animal の略とされるが, 和製英語.

UMA の一種チュパカブラ（Chupacabra）の想像図

有名税【ゆうめいぜい】a penalty of greatness; a price [toll] of being a celebrity.
◇それは一種の**有名税**さ. That's one of the costs you have to pay for being a big name.
◇それくらいのことは**有名税**だと思ってあきらめるんだね. You have to accept that something like that is a small price to pay for being famous [a celebrity].

指切り（げんまん）【ゆびきり（げんまん）】 a pledge between two people made by hooking little fingers together; a pinkie pledge.

◇指切りをする hook [link] *one's* little finger with . . . 's (as a token of a pledge).

◇指切りげんまん，うそついたら針千本飲ます．By hooking together our little fingers we make a promise; whoever breaks it must swallow a thousand needles.

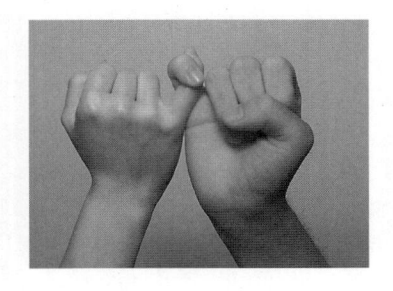

夢オチ【ゆめオチ】〔物語の結末ですべては夢だったと判明する落ち〕an "it was all a dream" ending; the ending of a story in which all turns out to have been a dream.

ゆるキャラ〔各種キャンペーン用の，ちょっと笑えるようなマスコットキャラクター〕a *yuru-kyara*; a mascot image used to promote an event, organization, etc., especially one seen as happy-go-lucky and endearing. ★⇨だつりょく

よ

ヨイショ 〔掛け声〕yo-ho!; yo-heave-ho!;〔人の機嫌を取っておだてること〕flattery.
◇ヨイショする flatter.

幼児体形[体型]【ようじたいけい】 a childish [prepubescent] figure.
◇(ぽちゃぽちゃの)**幼児体型**だ be plump; be chubby.

横入りする【よこはいりする】〔…に割り込む〕wedge (*oneself*) in [into . . .]; thrust [squeeze] *oneself* in [into . . .]; force [edge] *one's* way in; push in; edge into . . . ; break [cut, shove] in on . . . ;(強引に)muscle in on . . . ; intrude into [upon] . . . .
◇列に**横入りする** cut into the line; push in front of others; jump the queue.

寄せる【よせる】
◇**寄せ**て上げるブラ a push-up bra;〔リフトアップブラ〕a lift-up bra. ★⇨むね

予備軍【よびぐん】
◇失業**予備軍** the (growing) ranks of workers who are about to lose their jobs.
◇中年**予備軍** those who are nearing middle age.
◇糖尿病**予備軍** incipient diabetics.

呼び屋【よびや】〔海外から芸能人を招く人〕a promoter.

夜ごはん 【よるごはん】, 夜飯 【よるめし】 the evening meal; supper; dinner.

◇夜ごはんをスパゲッティにする eat [have] spaghetti for supper.
◇外で夜ごはんにする eat [take, have] supper out.
◇夜ごはんを抜いて寝る go to bed without eating.

ら

ライトノベル a novel for young adults; young adult fiction [literature].

ラウンドガール 〔ボクシングなどの試合で次のラウンド数を掲示するマスコットガール〕 a round card girl; a ring girl.

らしくない
◇あいつが自分からやるって言い出すなんて，なんか，らしくないよなあ． For him to come out and offer to do it—somehow, that's not like him.; I never would have expected him to volunteer to do it.

ラテ欄【ラテらん】〔新聞のラジオとテレビの番組表のページ〕 the TV and radio listings.

ラノベ ⇨ライトノベル

ラブコメ（ディー） a romantic comedy.

ラブホ（テル） a "love hotel"; a hotel catering to couples, renting rooms by the hour; a lovers'-rendezvous hotel; a sex hotel.

ラブラブ ★⇨りょうおもい
◇ラブラブのカップル a lovey-dovey couple; a passionate couple; a couple head over heels in love (with each other).
◇二人は今ラブラブだ． They are deeply [passionately, head over heels] in love (with each other).

ラン(ジェリー)パブ　a lingerie pub; a bar where the hostesses dress in lingerie.

り・る

リアクション
◇リアクション芸 comedy routine in which a comic does a slow burn, then erupts in a spluttering tirade in response to unfairness.

リーマン
〔サラリーマン〕a salaried worker [employee]; a white-collar worker; a company employee. ★日本のサラリーマンを指して a salaryman を使うこともある.

リカちゃん
〔着せ替え人形の商標〕Licca-chan.
◇リカちゃん人形 a Licca doll; a type of Japanese doll which can be dressed in different clothes.

リストラ
〔事業の再構築〕restructuring;〔首切り〕retrenchment (of employees as a result of restructuring).
◇リストラされる be fired [laid off].

リバースする
〔吐く〕vomit; throw up.

リバウンド
〔ダイエット後の〕rebound weight gain; gaining weight back.
◇リバウンドする put on weight again.
◇ダイエットをやめたら前よりもリバウンドした. When I stopped dieting I put on even more weight [my weight went up even higher] than before.

リフティング
◇リフティングをする juggle a soccer ball. ★英国では play

keepie uppie [keepy uppy] とも言う．lifting だけでは単に「(上に)あげること」のような意味になる．

リベンジする 〔…と対戦して雪辱を果たす〕win a rematch (against ...).

略奪【りゃくだつ】
◇**略奪愛** stealing another person's partner [lover, spouse].
◇**略奪婚**〔他人の恋人[婚約者]を奪って結婚すること〕a marriage where *one* steals another's sweetheart [betrothed].

両想い【りょうおもい】★⇨ラブラブ
◇**両想いになる** fall in love with each other.
◇男の子と**両想い**になれるおまじない love charm (that captures a man's heart).

ルーズソックス loose-fitting [baggy] white socks (worn by schoolgirls).

れ

レア
◇激レアもののお宝をゲットした I got my hands on a really rare item. ★⇨アイテム，おたからグッズ

レースクイーン
a "race queen"; a pretty young scantily dressed woman who adds female charm to auto races in Japan.

レディース
gang of women motorcyclists; woman motorcyclist who belongs to a gang.

レディースコミック
a women's comic.

連チャン【れんチャン】
◇今日は3連チャンで会議があった．Today I had three meetings in a row [one right after another].
◇昨日までの4連チャンの飲み会のあとではさすがに胃がもたれた．Going drinking four times in a short period through yesterday was enough to upset my stomach after all.

ろ

ローフード 〔自然の植物性食材を中心になるべく生に近い形で摂取する食生活〕eating a diet of chiefly raw vegetables and fruit.

ローリング族【ローリングぞく】〔車やバイクで曲がりくねった道などを暴走しスピードを競う集団〕car or motorcycle racers who compete on twisty roads.

ロケハン location hunting.
◇ロケハンに出かける go location hunting.

路駐【ろちゅう】〔路上駐車〕on-street [roadway] parking.

ロハス 〔健康と環境を大切にする生活様式〕LOHAS. ★ Lifestyles of Health and Sustainability の略.

ロムる 〔ネット掲示板で発言せず読むだけにする〕lurk (on a BBS). ★「ロム」は「読む(read)だけ(only)のメンバー(member)」の頭文字 ROM から. 英語の lurk は「表に出ず潜んで[隠れて]いる」の意で, この行為をする者を lurker と呼ぶ.

ロリ(コン) a man attracted to very young girls. ★⇨ショタコン
◇あいつはロリコンだ. He's into very young girls.; He has a thing for very young girls.
◇ロリコン系アート[イラスト] artwork portraying children in an erotic style.

◆ロリコン系雑誌 a *lolicon* magazine; a magazine [comic book] portraying children in an erotic style.

ロン毛【ロンげ】 (a (young) man with) long hair.

ロンドンブーツ 〔1970年代にロンドンで流行したかかとの高いブーツ〕"London" [flashy high-heeled] boots.

わ・を

訳あり【わけあり】
◇**訳有り品**〔特売の〕seconds; irregulars; imperfects; imperfect merchandise.
◇**訳有りな人** a person in a particular situation [with his own issues].
◇金を貸してくれないか，ちょっと**訳有り**なんだよ．Would you please lend me some money? Something's come up.
◇あのふたりはどうも**訳有り**らしい．It seems to me there's something (going on) between them.

わたし的【わたしてき】
◇**わたし的**には〔私としては〕as for me; as far as I'm concerned; for my part.

藁【わら】，（笑）【(かっこ)わらい】〔ネット上などで使う〕lol
★ laughing out loud（大爆笑している）の略．

ワリカン，割り勘
〔合計の人数割り〕an equal split;〔各自が自分の分を払う〕each paying for his own account;〔口語〕going Dutch.
◇**割り勘**でいこう．〔口語〕Let's split the tab.; Let's go Dutch.
◇**割り勘**にする split the cost; share the expenses.
◇プレゼント代を二人で**割り勘**にする go halves on a gift.
◇〔レジで〕**割り勘**にしてください．Separate checks, please.
◇部屋の家賃は4人で**割り勘**にした．The rent was split four ways.; The four of us split the room rent among us.

ワル 〔悪者〕a wicked [evil, bad] person; a bad lot;〔口語〕a baddie;〔不良〕a delinquent; a tough(ie); a rowdy; a hoodlum; a hooligan; a rough;〔不良グループ〕a bad lot. ★⇨ヤンキー
◇町のワル a street rowdy [tough]; a street rough.
◇ワルとつきあう mix [keep company] with delinquents [a bad lot].
◇ワルのたまり場 a hangout for delinquents.
◇彼は相当のワルだ．He's a very bad guy.
◇あの子はクラスで一番のワルだ．That boy [girl] is the most mischievous in the class.

悪乗り【わるのり】
◇悪乗りする overdo; go too far; take [carry] things too far (for others to accept); get carried away [too excited] (and spoil an event).
◇あいつは酒が入ると悪乗りする．He easily gets carried away [too excited] when drunk.

ワン切り【ワンぎり】〔電話をかけて1コールで切ること〕a one-ring hang-up call;〔それを利用した犯罪〕a one-ring callback scam.

ワンセグ 〔ワンセグメント放送の略；携帯電話で見られる放送〕one-segment broadcasting.

ワンパ，ワンパターン
◇ワンパな[の] one-track; single-track; following a single pattern.
◇ワンパターンな発想 a stereotyped idea
◇ワンパターンな人間 a person with only one approach to things [a one-track mind].
◇彼女の料理はワンパターンで，いつもカレーだ．She has only

one recipe, always curry. ★⇨おやくそく，ベタ

ヲタ(ク) ⇨オタク

装幀・ページデザイン
亀井 昌彦（株式会社シータス）

挿し絵
黒澤 優子

写真
Arashi & Mari
写真素材　足成
Hawk, Buddy, and Lavie

写真加工
矢治 由華子

俗語・流行語・業界用語…
なにげに使ってるコトバを英語にしてみる

いまどきのニホン語　和英辞典

2009 年 3 月 30 日　初版発行

KENKYUSHA

編著者	デイヴィッド・P・ダッチャー
編　者	研究社辞書編集部
発行者	関戸雅男
発行所	株式会社　研究社

〒102–8152　東京都千代田区富士見 2-11-3
電話　編集 03(3288)7711
　　　営業 03(3288)7777
振替　00150-9-26710
http://www.kenkyusha.co.jp

印刷所　研究社印刷株式会社

ISBN 978-4-7674-9104-2　C0582　PRINTED IN JAPAN